NUFFIELD
NATIONAL CURRICULUM
MATHEMATICS

Number and algebra 2

NC LEVEL 5

GCSE FOUNDATION

Heinemann

Project director: Peter Reynolds
Assistant director: Mike Cornelius
Project manager: Jan Hoare

Authors of this book
Rosemary Flower and Margaret Henshall with additional material by Graham Galtrey
Edited by Mike Cornelius

Heinemann Educational
a division of Heinemann Publishers (Oxford) Ltd,
Halley Court, Jordan Hill, Oxford, OX2 8EJ

OXFORD   LONDON   EDINBURGH
MADRID   ATHENS   BOLOGNA   PARIS
MELBOURNE   SYDNEY   AUCKLAND   SINGAPORE   TOKYO
IBADAN   NAIROBI   HARARE   GABORONE
PORTSMOUTH NH (USA)

First published 1995

95 96 97 98 10 9 8 7 6 5 4 3 2 1

ISBN 0 435 50544 0

Designed and typeset by Ken Vail Graphic Design
Illustrated by Rupert Besley, Paul Cookson, Joan Corlass, Nick Hawken,
Brian Hoskin, Mike Lacey, Nigel Paige, Peter Wilks, Graeme Morris (Ken Vail
Graphic Design)
Printed in Spain by Mateu Cromo, S.A. Pinto (Madrid)

Acknowledgements
The project and publishers gratefully acknowledge the contribution made by the late
Hilary Shuard.
For permission to reproduce the following photographs and copyright material the
authors and publishers would like to thank:
p. 28 Roger Scruton; p. 31 Science Photo Library/NASA; p. 35 Rex Features,
ZEFA; p. 55 Roger Scruton; p. 56 Collections/Anthea Sieveking; p. 62 Roger Scruton;
p. 71 C.M. Dixon; p. 79 Science Photo Library/Damien Lovegrove; P. 104
Collections/Neil Calladine.
Cover image: Science Photo Library/Melvin Prueitt
HMSO for permission to reproduce the National Curriculum level descriptions.

Every effort has been made to contact copyright holders of material published in this book.
Any omissions will be rectified in subsequent printings if notice is given to the publisher.

Cover picture
The spiral shape is related to a number pattern called the Fibonacci sequence.
This sequence is explored in Units 3 and 5.

About this book

This book is part of the Nuffield National Curriculum Mathematics series. It will help you learn mathematics and we hope you will enjoy using it.

How this book is organized

There are 12 units of work in this book. They are numbered Unit 1 to Unit 12. Each unit provides information for you to read and questions and activities for you to do.

The units are presented in short sections. Each section has a letter and a title. For example, Section B of Unit 2 has the title:

B Games with fraction cards

The questions and activities in Section B are numbered **B1**, **B2**, **B3** and so on to help you find them easily

The contents list on the next page shows you where each unit and section starts and tells you what mathematics they cover.

Symbols used in the Nuffield books

These symbols are shown in the margin of your book whenever you need worksheets, equipment or access to a computer:

this means you need Worksheet N2:4 from the Assessment and Resource Pack.

you need equipment listed between the lines

you need access to a computer and the software shown

Contents

UNIT 1 *Exploring fractions and decimals*

A Comparing fractions

The first part of this unit should remind you of things you already know about **fractions**.

Fractions are numbers such as $\frac{1}{3}$, $\frac{3}{4}$, $\frac{7}{10}$. The number on the bottom of the fraction (called the **denominator**) shows you into how many equal parts something is divided. The number on the top of the fraction (called the **numerator**) shows you how many of the smaller parts are counted.

For example, $\frac{7}{10}$ means divide something into 10 equal parts and then take 7 of these parts.

A1 Look at this rectangle:

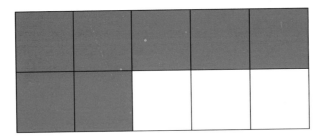

a What fraction is the shaded portion of the whole rectangle?

b What fraction is the unshaded portion?

c What is the sum of these two fractions?

You will often need to compare fractions. One way to do this is to write them as decimals. To do this divide the numerator (top number) by the denominator (bottom number) using a calculator.

For example, to find $\frac{3}{4}$ as a decimal calculate $3 \div 4$ and get 0.75.

A2 Rewrite the following as decimals:

$\frac{1}{4}$ $\frac{3}{10}$ $\frac{6}{25}$ $\frac{7}{20}$ $\frac{2}{5}$ $\frac{12}{25}$ $\frac{17}{68}$

A3 **a** Write down three examples of fractions – such as from a newspaper, a book or a shop window. Convert them to decimals and write each decimal next to its fraction.

   b Try some simple calculations with your fractions and decimals such as adding them together. Which did you find it is easier to do calculations with, fractions or decimals? Explain your choice.

A4 **a** Use your calculator to find these fractions as decimals:

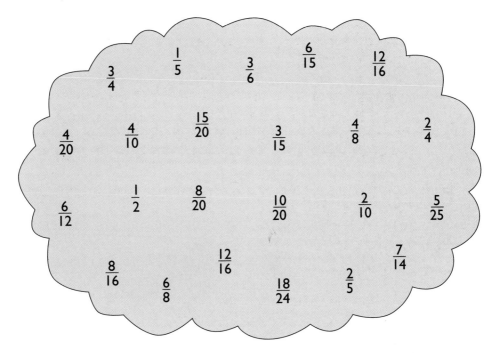

$$\frac{3}{4} \quad \frac{1}{5} \quad \frac{3}{6} \quad \frac{6}{15} \quad \frac{12}{16}$$

$$\frac{4}{20} \quad \frac{4}{10} \quad \frac{15}{20} \quad \frac{3}{15} \quad \frac{4}{8} \quad \frac{2}{4}$$

$$\frac{6}{12} \quad \frac{1}{2} \quad \frac{8}{20} \quad \frac{10}{20} \quad \frac{2}{10} \quad \frac{5}{25}$$

$$\frac{8}{16} \quad \frac{6}{8} \quad \frac{12}{16} \quad \frac{18}{24} \quad \frac{2}{5} \quad \frac{7}{14}$$

   b List any fractions which have the *same* decimal as each other. Fractions like these are called **equivalent fractions**.

   c Fractions that are equivalent represent the same amount. This diagram shows that $\frac{1}{4}$, $\frac{2}{8}$, $\frac{4}{16}$ are equivalent. Write down the decimal which represents each of them.

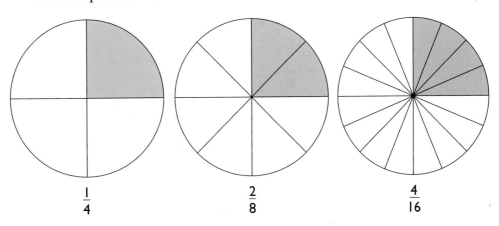

$$\frac{1}{4} \qquad\qquad \frac{2}{8} \qquad\qquad \frac{4}{16}$$

BASIC

A5 Here is a **BASIC** computer program to work out decimals and equivalent fractions:

```
10 FOR N = 1 TO 20
20 LET T = 1
30 LET B = 5
40 LET T = N*T
50 LET B = N*B
60 LET D = T/B
70 PRINT T; "/"; B; "="; D
80 NEXT N
```

a If you can, use a computer to run the program. If not, try to work out what happens for yourself. What does the program do?

b What do T, B and D stand for?

A6 Write your own program to print out the family of fractions equivalent to $\frac{1}{4}$.

Check that your program produces the following fractions:

$\frac{1}{4}$ $\frac{2}{8}$ $\frac{3}{12}$ $\frac{4}{16}$ $\frac{5}{20}$ $\frac{6}{24}$ $\frac{7}{28}$ $\frac{9}{36}$ $\frac{10}{40}$ … and so on.

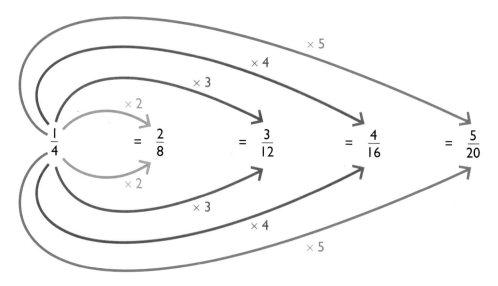

These are all equivalent to $\frac{1}{4}$ as all give 0.25 when the numerator is divided by the denominator.

A7 **a** Write down six fractions equivalent to $\frac{4}{5}$.

b Use your calculator to check that these fractions all give the same decimal when you divide the numerator by the denominator.

A8 Copy and complete these sets of equivalent fractions and finally write numerator/denominator as a decimal:

a $\frac{3}{5} = \frac{\square}{10} = \frac{9}{\square} = \frac{\square}{\square} = \frac{15}{25} = \frac{\square}{30} = \frac{21}{\square} = \frac{\square}{40}$

numerator/denominator =

b $\frac{1}{10} = \frac{2}{\square} = \frac{\square}{30} = \frac{\square}{\square} = \frac{5}{50} = \frac{\square}{60} = \frac{7}{\square} = \frac{\square}{80} = \frac{\square}{90}$

numerator/denominator =

c $\frac{7}{10} = \frac{\square}{20} = \frac{21}{\square} = \frac{28}{40} = \frac{\square}{50} = \frac{\square}{\square} = \frac{49}{\square} = \frac{\square}{80}$

numerator/denominator =

d $\frac{2}{5} = \frac{4}{\square} = \frac{\square}{15} = \frac{\square}{\square} = \frac{10}{25} = \frac{12}{\square} = \frac{\square}{\square} = \frac{\square}{40}$

numerator/denominator =

e $\frac{3}{8} = \frac{\square}{16} = \frac{9}{\square} = \frac{\square}{\square} = \frac{\square}{40} = \frac{18}{\square} = \frac{\square}{56} = \frac{24}{\square}$

numerator/denominator =

A9 **a** For each of these diagrams write down:

i the shaded fraction

ii the unshaded fraction.

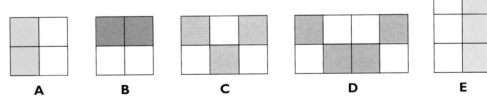

    A   **B**   **C**   **D**   **E**

b What is the simplest way of writing each of these fractions?

A10 Describe an example from everyday life where you might need to use equivalent fractions.

A11 **a** Look at the diagrams below. What fraction of each one is shaded?

b Make a list of the fractions represented by the shaded areas and find out whether there are any equivalent fractions among them.

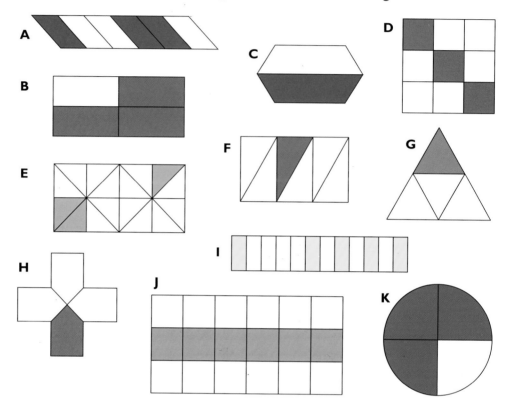

A12 Use this fraction table to find equivalent fractions for $\frac{1}{2}$, $\frac{1}{3}$ and $\frac{1}{4}$.

1 whole																							
$\frac{1}{2}$												$\frac{1}{2}$											
$\frac{1}{3}$								$\frac{1}{3}$								$\frac{1}{3}$							
$\frac{1}{4}$						$\frac{1}{4}$						$\frac{1}{4}$						$\frac{1}{4}$					
$\frac{1}{6}$				$\frac{1}{6}$				$\frac{1}{6}$				$\frac{1}{6}$				$\frac{1}{6}$				$\frac{1}{6}$			
$\frac{1}{12}$		$\frac{1}{12}$		$\frac{1}{12}$		$\frac{1}{12}$		$\frac{1}{12}$		$\frac{1}{12}$		$\frac{1}{12}$		$\frac{1}{12}$		$\frac{1}{12}$		$\frac{1}{12}$		$\frac{1}{12}$		$\frac{1}{12}$	
$\frac{1}{24}$	$\frac{1}{24}$	$\frac{1}{24}$	$\frac{1}{24}$	$\frac{1}{24}$	$\frac{1}{24}$	$\frac{1}{24}$	$\frac{1}{24}$	$\frac{1}{24}$	$\frac{1}{24}$	$\frac{1}{24}$	$\frac{1}{24}$	$\frac{1}{24}$	$\frac{1}{24}$	$\frac{1}{24}$	$\frac{1}{24}$	$\frac{1}{24}$	$\frac{1}{24}$	$\frac{1}{24}$	$\frac{1}{24}$	$\frac{1}{24}$	$\frac{1}{24}$	$\frac{1}{24}$	$\frac{1}{24}$

A13 Draw your own fraction tables to show equivalents for:

a $\frac{1}{2}$ $\frac{1}{5}$ $\frac{1}{10}$ $\frac{1}{20}$ $\frac{1}{40}$

b $\frac{1}{2}$ $\frac{1}{4}$ $\frac{1}{8}$ $\frac{1}{16}$ $\frac{1}{32}$

B Graphs and equivalent fractions

N2:1

B1 **a** On centimetre squared paper draw the two axes shown below, or use worksheet N2:1. Label the horizontal axis 'Numerator' and the vertical axis 'Denominator'. Use a scale of 1 cm to one unit on each axis.

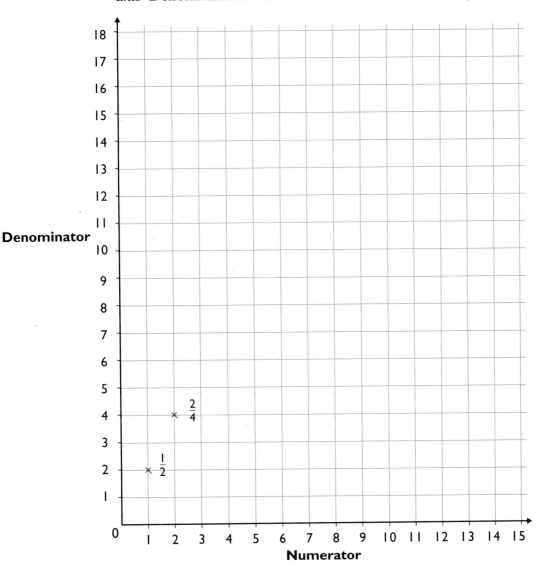

b Using your results from questions **A12** and **A13**, plot the following fractions and their equivalents on your graph:

$\frac{1}{2}$ $\frac{1}{3}$ $\frac{1}{4}$ $\frac{1}{5}$ ($\frac{1}{2}$ and $\frac{2}{4}$ have already been done for you.)

c Draw a straight line from the point 0 to each fraction in turn.

d What do you notice about fractions that fit on to the same line?

e Show each set of equivalent fractions using a different colour.

Here is another method of finding equivalent fractions. Look carefully at the graph below. Notice that this time the Denominator and Numerator are on different axes.

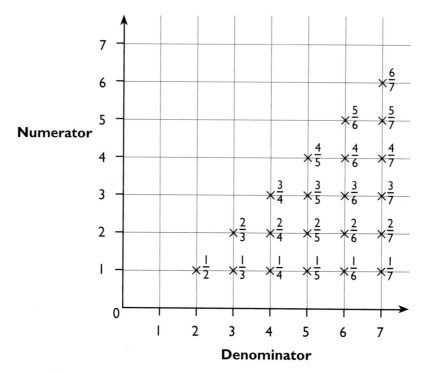

To find fractions in order of size, put your ruler on 0 and place it along the horizontal axis. Slowly turn the ruler anticlockwise, keeping one end on 0. The first fraction you come to is $\frac{1}{7}$ because this is the smallest. Then you get $\frac{1}{6}$, $\frac{1}{5}$, $\frac{1}{4}$, $\frac{1}{3}$ but notice that at $\frac{1}{3}$ the ruler also passes through another fraction. Which fraction is it? What can you say about these two fractions?

B2 **a** Using centimetre squared paper, with the long side along the bottom, draw two axes. Mark the horizontal axis 'Denominator' with a scale from 0 to 13. Mark the vertical axis 'Numerator' with a scale from 0 to 9. Use 2 cm for one unit on both axes. Mark in all the fractions you can, as on the previous graph.

   b Use your graph to list all the fractions in order of size, starting with the smallest.

   c Write down as many sets of equivalent fractions as you can.

C Decimals

Most of the fractions converted to decimals so far have had one, two or three digits after the decimal point, for example:

$\frac{1}{2} = 0.5$ $\frac{1}{5} = 0.2$ $\frac{1}{4} = 0.25$ $\frac{1}{8} = 0.125$

Fractions like this produce decimals which are said to **terminate**.
(What is meant by saying a train 'terminates' at a station?)

C1 **a** Use your calculator, or the following program, to see what happens to some other fractions when they are changed to decimals. Use the computer if you can, as your calculator may not give sufficient decimal places.

```
10 INPUT T
20 INPUT B
30 LET D = T/B
40 PRINT T; "/"; B; "="; D
```

b Write each of these fractions as decimals:

$\frac{1}{7}$ $\frac{1}{3}$ $\frac{1}{9}$ $\frac{1}{13}$ $\frac{1}{14}$ $\frac{2}{7}$ $\frac{3}{7}$ $\frac{4}{7}$ $\frac{5}{7}$ $\frac{6}{7}$

What do you notice about the results?

c Write the decimals for $\frac{1}{7}$ $\frac{2}{7}$ $\frac{3}{7}$ $\frac{4}{7}$ $\frac{5}{7}$ $\frac{6}{7}$ one above the other.
What do you notice?

C2   Work out the decimals for $\frac{1}{9}$ $\frac{2}{9}$ $\frac{3}{9}$ ...
What pattern can you see?

C3   Work out the decimals for $\frac{1}{11}$ $\frac{2}{11}$ $\frac{3}{11}$ ...
What pattern do they show?

You should have found that some decimals from fractions repeat the
same pattern of digits over and over again. Decimals like this are called
recurring decimals. 'Recurring' means 'repeating'.

For example, $\frac{1}{3}$ = 0.$\dot{3}$33333333 ... this is written as 0.$\dot{3}$

The dot is used to show that the digit 3 is repeated. Here is another example:

0.$\dot{1}\dot{8}$ = 0.1818181818 ... = $\frac{2}{11}$

When a *group* of digits are repeated two dots are used, for example:

$\frac{1}{7}$ = 0.142857142857142857 ... this is written as 0.$\dot{1}$4285$\dot{7}$

C4   Write the following fractions as decimals using the dot to show that
they recur:

$\frac{2}{3}$ $\frac{1}{9}$ $\frac{2}{14}$ $\frac{3}{14}$ $\frac{4}{14}$ $\frac{5}{14}$

Some calculators correct the last digit on the display in recurring
decimals. For example:

$\frac{2}{3}$ = 0.6666666666 ... = 0.$\dot{6}$

but if you enter 2 ÷ 3 your calculator may display this as 0.66666667

Find out if your calculator operates like this.

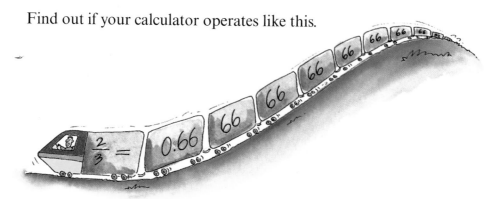

C5   **a**   Copy this table:

F	T or R	F	T or R	F	T or R	F	T or R	F	T or R
$\frac{1}{2}$	T								
$\frac{1}{3}$	R	$\frac{2}{3}$	R						
$\frac{1}{4}$	T	$\frac{2}{4}$							
$\frac{1}{5}$	T	$\frac{2}{5}$		$\frac{3}{4}$					
$\frac{1}{6}$		$\frac{2}{6}$		$\frac{3}{5}$		$\frac{4}{5}$			
$\frac{1}{7}$		$\frac{2}{7}$		$\frac{3}{6}$		$\frac{4}{6}$		$\frac{5}{6}$	
$\frac{1}{8}$		$\frac{2}{8}$		$\frac{3}{7}$		$\frac{4}{7}$		$\frac{5}{7}$	
$\frac{1}{9}$		$\frac{2}{9}$		$\frac{3}{8}$		$\frac{4}{8}$		$\frac{5}{8}$	
$\frac{1}{10}$		$\frac{2}{10}$		$\frac{3}{9}$		$\frac{4}{9}$		$\frac{5}{9}$	
$\frac{1}{11}$		$\frac{2}{11}$		$\frac{3}{10}$		$\frac{4}{10}$		$\frac{5}{10}$	
$\frac{1}{12}$		$\frac{2}{12}$		$\frac{3}{11}$		$\frac{4}{11}$		$\frac{5}{11}$	
$\frac{1}{13}$		$\frac{2}{13}$		$\frac{3}{12}$		$\frac{4}{12}$		$\frac{5}{12}$	
$\frac{1}{14}$		$\frac{2}{14}$		$\frac{3}{13}$		$\frac{4}{13}$		$\frac{5}{13}$	
$\frac{1}{15}$		$\frac{2}{15}$		$\frac{3}{14}$		$\frac{4}{14}$		$\frac{5}{14}$	
$\frac{1}{16}$		$\frac{2}{16}$		$\frac{3}{15}$		$\frac{4}{15}$		$\frac{5}{15}$	
$\frac{1}{17}$		$\frac{2}{17}$		$\frac{3}{16}$		$\frac{4}{16}$		$\frac{5}{16}$	
$\frac{1}{18}$		$\frac{2}{18}$		$\frac{3}{17}$		$\frac{4}{17}$		$\frac{5}{17}$	
$\frac{1}{19}$		$\frac{2}{19}$		$\frac{3}{18}$		$\frac{4}{18}$		$\frac{5}{18}$	
$\frac{1}{20}$		$\frac{2}{20}$		$\frac{3}{19}$		$\frac{4}{19}$		$\frac{5}{19}$	
$\frac{1}{21}$		$\frac{2}{21}$		$\frac{3}{20}$		$\frac{4}{20}$		$\frac{5}{20}$	
$\frac{1}{22}$		$\frac{2}{22}$		$\frac{3}{21}$		$\frac{4}{21}$		$\frac{5}{21}$	
$\frac{1}{23}$		$\frac{2}{23}$		$\frac{3}{22}$		$\frac{4}{22}$		$\frac{5}{22}$	
$\frac{1}{24}$		$\frac{2}{24}$		$\frac{3}{23}$		$\frac{4}{23}$		$\frac{5}{23}$	
$\frac{1}{25}$		$\frac{2}{25}$		$\frac{3}{24}$		$\frac{4}{24}$		$\frac{5}{24}$	
				$\frac{3}{25}$		$\frac{4}{25}$		$\frac{5}{25}$	

F = Fraction   T = Terminating decimal   R = recurring decimal

    b   Using the computer or your calculator find out for each fraction whether it terminates or recurs and complete the table.

    c   Try to find a rule which predicts whether a fraction will terminate or recur.

C6   On your calculator you will find a key marked   ☑ .

Find $\sqrt{2}$ $\sqrt{3}$ $\sqrt{4}$ $\sqrt{5}$ $\sqrt{6}$ $\sqrt{7}$ $\sqrt{8}$ and $\sqrt{9}$.

What do you notice about the answers you get? What do you think will be the next one to give a whole number?

UNIT 2 *Using fractions*

large sheets
of I cm
squared
paper
metre ruler

A Putting fractions in their places

A1 **a** Cut 25 cm wide strips from a large sheet of centimetre squared paper. Stick them together to form a strip of paper 25 cm by about 110 cm. Draw a straight line, longer than 1 metre, approximately in the middle of the strip of paper.

  b Mark two points on the line *exactly* 1 metre apart and label them 0 and 1.

  c Starting at 0, mark points on your line at 1 cm intervals.

  d Now label your points as **fractions**. Start by labelling the middle point of the line as a half ($\frac{1}{2}$) and then label the quarters and the tenths, as shown below.

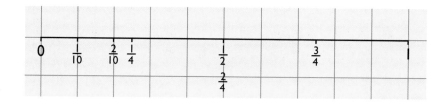

  e Now try to label all the other points. You will need to include fifths, twentieths, twenty-fifths, fiftieths and hundredths. Some points will have more than one label.

  f How many labels have you put for the mid-point of the line (for example: $\frac{1}{2}$, $\frac{10}{20}$, $\frac{50}{100}$,…)? Make a list of your mid-point labels.

  (Note: you need to retain the line prepared in question **A1** for use throughout the work of Unit 2.)

A2 **a** Make a list of all the points on your line which have more than one label.

  b How many points can you find with six labels?

  c What can you say about points with only one label?

Start at 0 on your line and move along it to the point $\frac{10}{25}$. Then from $\frac{10}{25}$ move a distance of $\frac{1}{5}$. You should reach $\frac{30}{50}$.

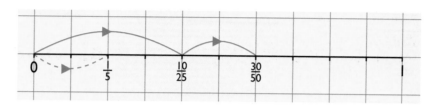

You could write this journey as a **fraction sum** as follows:

$\frac{10}{25} + \frac{1}{5} = \frac{30}{50}$

A3 **a** Use equivalent fractions to show that this fraction sum is true. Make yourself some strips of paper equal in length to the fractions used and show that the first two strips together have the same length as the third one.

b Rewrite the journey from 0 to $\frac{30}{50}$ in three other ways and again check your answers by making paper strips for the fractions involved.

c Make up three journeys from 0 to $\frac{30}{50}$ stopping at $\frac{1}{10}$ on the way. Write each journey as a fraction sum.

A4 This diagram represents another journey.

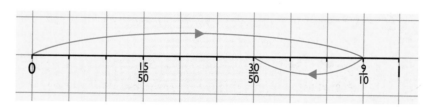

a Write down a fraction equation to represent the journey and use equivalent fractions to show that your equation is true.

b Make up five more journeys which allow you to finish at $\frac{30}{50}$ after first going past $\frac{30}{50}$ and then doubling back. Record your answers and check them using equivalent fractions.

A5   This diagram shows a journey of three lots of $\frac{1}{10}$.

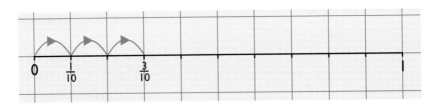

Draw diagrams of your own to show journeys which could be recorded using these words:

a   lots of

b   multiplied by

c   half of

d   split equally into five

e   shared equally into four.

Write a fraction sum for each journey.

A6

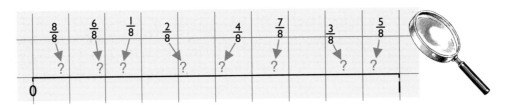

a   Where should you put members of the eighths family ($\frac{1}{8}$, $\frac{2}{8}$, $\frac{3}{8}$, $\frac{4}{8}$, $\frac{5}{8}$, $\frac{6}{8}$, $\frac{7}{8}$, $\frac{8}{8}$) on your line?
(Note: you are *not* allowed to use fractions like $\frac{12.5}{100}$. There must only be whole numbers on the top and bottom of the fractions.)

b   Mark the eighths family on your line. What other name could you give to $\frac{1}{8}$?

A7

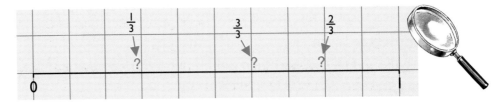

a   Now see if you can place the thirds family ($\frac{1}{3}$, $\frac{2}{3}$, $\frac{3}{3}$). Mark them on your line.

b   How would you describe the positions of $\frac{1}{3}$ and $\frac{2}{3}$ on the line?

c   Can you find other ways to label $\frac{1}{3}$ and $\frac{2}{3}$?

B Games with fraction cards

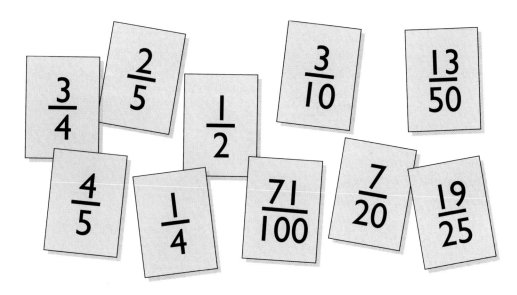

N2:2

You need a set of ten fraction cards from Worksheet N2:2

B1 a Shuffle the fraction cards and deal yourself five cards. Sort the fractions cards into size order and place them side-by-side with the lowest value fraction on the left and the highest on the right. Check your order is correct using the number line prepared in question **A1**.

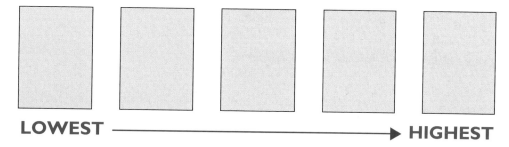

LOWEST ⟶ HIGHEST

b Repeat part **a** ten times and see how many times you can get all five cards in the correct order. Check your order each time using your number line.

c Now deal yourself *ten* cards and place them in order, once again checking with your number line.

blank cards **B2** On a set of ten blank cards write ten fractions of your own choice. Swap your cards with a set produced by a friend and see if each of you can put the other person's cards in the correct order.

Check, if necessary, using your number line.

C Putting things in order

Do you know these?

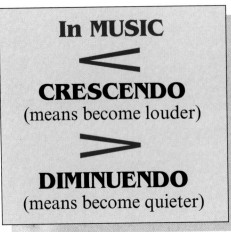
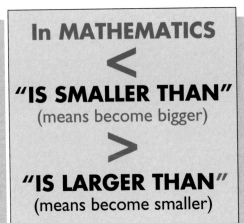

So   "Is $\frac{1}{2} > \frac{1}{4}$?"   means   "Is $\frac{1}{2}$ greater than $\frac{1}{4}$?

C1 **a** Is $\frac{17}{20} > \frac{19}{25}$? Use the number line you prepared in question **A1** to help you.

You should find that both fractions belong to the hundredths family:

$\frac{17}{20} = \frac{85}{100}$ and $\frac{19}{25} = \frac{76}{100}$

Is it clear which is bigger now?

b Is $\frac{3}{50} < \frac{2}{20}$?

C2 Put the correct symbol, either <, = or >, between the fractions in each of the following. Use the number line prepared in question **A1** to help you.

a $\frac{3}{10}$ $\frac{1}{5}$ **b** $\frac{2}{5}$ $\frac{1}{2}$ **c** $\frac{3}{4}$ $\frac{3}{5}$

d $\frac{38}{100}$ $\frac{19}{50}$ **e** $\frac{71}{100}$ $\frac{3}{4}$ **f** $\frac{4}{25}$ $\frac{1}{20}$

g $\frac{24}{25}$ $\frac{19}{20}$ **h** $\frac{24}{50}$ $\frac{1}{2}$ $\frac{11}{20}$ **i** $\frac{23}{25}$ $\frac{19}{20}$ $\frac{49}{50}$

j $\frac{17}{20}$ $\frac{4}{5}$ $\frac{3}{4}$ **k** $\frac{3}{8}$ $\frac{1}{2}$ **l** $\frac{1}{3}$ $\frac{1}{4}$

m $\frac{3}{4}$ $\frac{2}{3}$ **n** $\frac{5}{8}$ $\frac{7}{10}$ **o** $\frac{17}{25}$ $\frac{2}{3}$ $\frac{13}{20}$

C3 Arrange these in order of size and put the correct symbol between the fractions in each of the following:

a $\frac{1}{10}$ $\frac{7}{20}$ $\frac{3}{100}$ $\frac{9}{25}$ **b** $\frac{19}{50}$ $\frac{11}{20}$ $\frac{1}{3}$ $\frac{3}{8}$ **c** $\frac{5}{8}$ $\frac{47}{50}$ $\frac{17}{20}$ $\frac{23}{25}$ $\frac{2}{3}$

C4 Look at this sequence of fractions:

$\frac{1}{2}$ $\frac{2}{3}$ $\frac{3}{4}$ $\frac{4}{5}$ ...

   a Which fraction comes next?

   b Write down the next ten fractions in the sequence.

   c What do you think will happen if you continue the sequence a long time?

C5

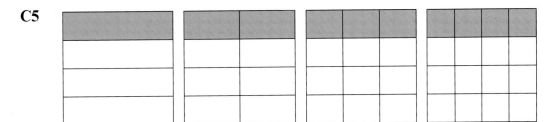

The diagrams above show the first four fractions equivalent to $\frac{1}{4}$.
Draw the next two diagrams in this set.

C6 Draw a set of diagrams for the first five fractions equivalent to:

   a $\frac{1}{3}$ **b** $\frac{2}{3}$ **c** $\frac{1}{5}$

C7 **a** Write down the first six fractions equivalent to $\frac{4}{5}$.

   b What do you notice about the numerators (top numbers) and denominators (bottom numbers)? Describe how you change one fraction to another.

C8 Fill in the missing numbers. (Hint: you may find your answers to question C7 on changing fractions useful here.)

   a $\frac{3}{4} = \frac{\square}{8}$ **b** $\frac{3}{5} = \frac{\square}{30}$ **c** $\frac{7}{20} = \frac{21}{\square}$

   d $\frac{\square}{8} = \frac{56}{64}$ **e** $\frac{7}{10} = \frac{\square}{100} = \frac{700}{\square} = \frac{7000}{\square}$ **f** $\frac{7}{8} = \frac{49}{\square} = \frac{\square}{240} = \frac{357}{\square}$

C9 Write down how you can find missing numbers from equivalent fractions quickly.

D Addition and subtraction

D1 **a** Use your number line from question **A1** to check that:

$$\tfrac{1}{4} + \tfrac{1}{5} = \tfrac{9}{20}$$

   b Check your answer by converting $\tfrac{1}{4}$ and $\tfrac{1}{5}$ to twentieths.

   c To which *other* family of fractions do $\tfrac{1}{4}$ and $\tfrac{1}{5}$ belong? Use this family to find an alternative answer. Is the answer equivalent to $\tfrac{9}{20}$?

D2 Use two different methods to work out: $\tfrac{1}{4} - \tfrac{1}{5}$

D3 Use your number line to work out the following (you may find it helpful to make paper number strips to represent the fractions):

   a $\tfrac{7}{10} + \tfrac{2}{5}$ **b** $\tfrac{3}{8} + \tfrac{1}{5}$ **c** $\tfrac{7}{8} - \tfrac{1}{2}$

   d $\tfrac{5}{8} + \tfrac{7}{10}$ **e** $\tfrac{2}{3} + \tfrac{5}{6}$ **f** $\tfrac{7}{9} - \tfrac{1}{3}$

   g $\tfrac{3}{5} + \tfrac{3}{7}$ **h** $\tfrac{3}{4} + \tfrac{9}{10}$

   i $\tfrac{1}{2} + \tfrac{3}{4} + \tfrac{5}{6}$ **j** $\tfrac{5}{4} - \tfrac{3}{5}$

E Multiplication and division

E1 Use your number line from question **A1** to do these. What do you notice?

   a 2 lots of $\tfrac{3}{10}$ **b** 3 lots of $\tfrac{2}{10}$ **c** 6 lots of $\tfrac{1}{10}$

   d $\tfrac{3}{10} \times 2$ **e** $2 \times \tfrac{3}{10}$ **f** $3 \times \tfrac{2}{10}$

   g $\tfrac{3}{10} \times \tfrac{2}{1}$ **h** $6 \times \tfrac{1}{10}$ **i** $\tfrac{2}{10} \times \tfrac{3}{1}$

E2 Here is a diagram which shows that: $\frac{1}{2}$ of $\frac{1}{5} = \frac{1}{10}$

Work out the following, using diagrams to help you:

a $\frac{1}{4}$ of $\frac{1}{5}$ **b** $\frac{1}{4}$ of $\frac{3}{5}$ **c** $\frac{3}{4}$ of $\frac{3}{5}$

d 9 lots of ($\frac{1}{4}$ of $\frac{1}{5}$)   **e** 9 lots of $\frac{1}{20}$ **f** 3 lots of ($\frac{1}{4}$ of $\frac{3}{5}$)

E3 Is 3 lots of $\frac{5}{8}$ the same as 5 lots of $\frac{3}{8}$?

E4 What fraction of this rectangle is shaded:

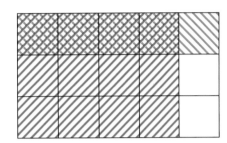

   a red

   b green

   c both colours?

E5 Calculate:

a $\frac{1}{4}$ of $\frac{1}{2}$ **b** $\frac{3}{4}$ of 4   **c** $\frac{2}{5}$ of $\frac{1}{2}$ **d** $\frac{4}{5}$ of $\frac{3}{4}$

e $\frac{2}{5}$ of $1\frac{1}{2}$ **f** $\frac{1}{4}$ of $2\frac{1}{2}$ **g** $3 \times \frac{2}{5}$ **h** $4 \times \frac{7}{8}$

i $\frac{7}{2} \times \frac{4}{8}$ **j** $3\frac{1}{2} \times \frac{4}{7}$

E6 Use your number line from question **A1** to answer the following questions.

   a How many quarters are there in $\frac{3}{4}$?

   b How many tenths are there in $\frac{1}{2}$?

   c How many thirds are there in 2?

   d How many lots of three tenths are there in $1\frac{1}{2}$?

E7 Work out:

a $\frac{3}{4} \div \frac{1}{4}$ **b** $\frac{1}{2} \div \frac{1}{10}$ **c** $2 \div \frac{1}{3}$ **d** $1\frac{1}{2} \div \frac{3}{10}$

Compare your answers with question **E6**!

E8 Work out the following:

   a How many halves are there in 3?   **b** $3 \div \frac{1}{2}$

   c $5 \div \frac{1}{2}$ **d** $\frac{7}{10} \div \frac{1}{10}$

   e How many tenths are there in $\frac{9}{10}$?   **f** $\frac{9}{10} \div \frac{3}{10}$ **g** $\frac{9}{10} \div 3$

F **Fractions and decimals**

F1   Copy and complete the following:

a   0.5 means five *tenths* of a whole unit

b   0.03 means _____

c   0.001 means _____

d   0.25 means   2 *tenths* and
    5 _____
    or 25 *hundredths*

e   0.125 means   1 _____ and
    2 _____ and
    5 _____
    or 125 *thousandths*.

F2   Make a table with column headings like these:

hundreds	tens	units	.	tenths	hundredths	thousandths
	2	7	.	2	4	6

Write the following numbers in your table. The first one has been done for you.

a 27.246   b 30.5   c 1.25   d 0.625   e 7   f 4.05

g 29.105   h 138   i 564.9   j 12.008   k 190.1   l 100.001

F3   There are many ways of writing $\frac{1}{2}$. For example: $\frac{5}{10}$ $\frac{50}{100}$ …

Write down three other ways.

Now write $\frac{5}{10}$ $\frac{50}{100}$ $\frac{500}{1000}$ as *decimals*.

F4   Write the following as *fractions*:

a   0.3 0.30 0.300

b   0.01 0.010 0.0100

c   0.7 0.70 0.700

F5 Write these fractions as *decimals*:

   a $\frac{1}{10}$ $\frac{10}{100}$ $\frac{100}{1000}$

   b $\frac{25}{100}$ $\frac{250}{1000}$ $\frac{2500}{10000}$

   c $\frac{7}{10}$ $\frac{70}{100}$ $\frac{700}{1000}$

You should notice that adding extra zeros *after* the decimal ends makes no difference to its actual value. So:

$0.6 = 0.60 = 0.600 = 0.6000$ … and so on.

F6 Write 3 500 060 in words. Now try to write 0.123 456 in words.

You should find yourself using 'tenths', 'hundredths', 'thousandths', 'ten thousandths', 'hundred thousandths' and 'millionths'.

F7 Describe the following in words:

   a 0.000 1   **b** 0.000 01   **c** 0.000 001   **d** 0.100 100

   e 0.000 123   **f** 0.234 567   **g** 0.010 101   **h** 0.001 000

F8 Change these fractions to decimals:

   a $\frac{1}{1000}$ **b** $\frac{1}{10\,000}$ **c** $\frac{1}{100\,000}$ **d** $\frac{1}{1\,000\,000}$ **e** $\frac{10}{1\,000\,000}$

   f $\frac{100}{100\,000}$ **g** $\frac{5}{1\,000\,000}$ **h** $\frac{250}{1\,000\,000}$ **i** $\frac{7}{10\,000}$

F9 How long have you been alive in years, in months and in days? Work out (in appropriate units) the following fractions of your lifetime so far:

   a $\frac{1}{10}$ **b** $\frac{1}{100}$ **c** $\frac{1}{1000}$

   d $\frac{1}{10\,000}$ **e** $\frac{100}{100\,000}$ **f** $\frac{1}{1\,000\,000}$

F10 Using a calculator, find *half* of the following numbers:

   a 1   **b** a tenth   **c** a hundredth   **d** a thousandth   **e** a millionth.

F11 Put these numbers in order of size, with the largest number first:

   0.0075   7 thousandths   75 millionths   0.000 75   0.000 007 5

UNIT 3 *Numbers, patterns and powers*

A The Cayley table

Ben has been given a problem to solve for homework. He has been told that to solve it he can only use the following:

● multiplication facts up to 5×5

● addition sums.

He can only use his calculator to check his answers.

The problem is how much change would he receive from £60 if he bought seven tee shirts at £8 each?

So, Ben needs to work out 7×8 but is restricted to use only the multiplication facts up to 5×5 and addition sums.

A1 See if you can find a way to get an answer using Ben's restrictions. Record your method.

A2 Here is Ben's solution. Explain how it works.

$7 = 2 + 5$

$8 = 3 + 5$

×	2	+	5	7
3	6		15	21
+				+
5	10		25	35
8				56

A3   Repeat Ben's method using $3 + 4$ instead of $2 + 5$. Do you get the same answer?

A4   If 7 and 8 are each split into the sum of two numbers, list all the possible ways of calculating 7×8. How many of the ways you find would Ben be able to use? (Remember he can only use multiplications up to 5×5.)

A5   Check for yourself all the methods Ben could use and make sure you always get the same answer!

Ben has become fascinated by this method of calculation. He knows that there are 12 ways of using two numbers to split up 7 and 8. He now wonders how many different ways there might be if there were no restrictions on the number of parts into which 7 and 8 were split.

A6   How many ways do you think there are?
Here are two ways:

×	1	+	2	+	2	+	3	8
1	1		2		2		3	8
+								+
2	2		4		4		6	16
+								+
4	4		8		8		12	32
7								56

×	1	+	1	+	1	+	1	+	2	+	2	8
1	1		1		1		1		2		2	8
+												+
2	2		2		2		2		4		4	16
+												+
2	2		2		2		2		4		4	16
+												+
2	2		2		2		2		4		4	16
7												56

Write down five more.

Ben found that there were over 300 different ways of doing the sum like this! How many did you find?

Tables like the ones Ben used are called **Cayley tables**. They were devised by Arthur Cayley, an English mathematician who was born in 1821.

A7   Use six different Cayley tables to work out 6 × 9 using the same restrictions as before.

A8   Use a Cayley table method to work out the following:

   a   12 × 9   **b**   16 × 8   **c**   17 × 12

   d   23 × 17   **e**   19 × 24

   Check your answers with a calculator.

A9   Repeat the calculations in question **A8** using any method which you have used before. Try to explain how your method works.

Do you know the 17 and 23 times tables? Only a few people can calculate 23 × 17 without a calculator or pencil and paper. Some people work it out in their heads:

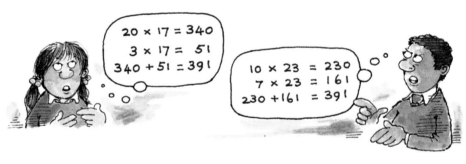

These methods are similar to Cayley tables.

A10   Write the two methods above in Cayley table form.

A11   Do these calculations in your head and write down the answers:

   a 10 × 17   **b** 30 × 7   **c** 30 × 70   **d** 300 × 7

   e 300 × 70   **f** 100 × 30 × 70   **g** 3000 × 50 000

A12   Using your calculator, investigate what happens to numbers when you multiply by 10 or multiples of 10. Write a summary of your findings.

A13   Do the following in your head and write down the answers:

   a 10×7 **b** 30×7 **c** 400×7

   d 10×30 **e** 40×20 **f** 30×700

   g 400×200 **h** 500×4000 **i** $200 \times 30 \times 7$

   j $300 \times 90 \times 2000$

   Check your answers with a calculator.

A14   Use Cayley tables (or any other method) to do the following:
   (Try to find the quickest possible method.)

   a 9×37 **b** 17×36 **c** 23×115

   d 229×31 **e** 307×49 **f** 523×67

   Check your answers with a calculator.

A15   Calculate these, first using Cayley tables and then checking with a calculator:

   a 329×2367 **b** 597×1234 **c** 3297×2637

A16   **a**   Throw a dice six times and record the numbers thrown, for example:

   Then use Cayley tables to do the multiplication you get by making
   your scores into two 3-digit numbers, for example:

   b   Repeat part **a** five times.

The Pierrot's puzzle

A17   The Pierrot in the picture is pretending to be a multiplication sign.
What is the answer to the sum?
Look carefully at the digits in the answer. What do you notice?

The Pierrot's puzzle is to take four digits, all different, and arrange them
so that when you multiply you get the same digits in the answer.

You can put two digits on each side of the Pierrot or three digits on one
side and one digit on the other. You have already solved one puzzle in
question **A17:** $15 \times 93 = 1395$.

A18   **a**   Here are three solutions to Pierrot puzzles, each with one digit
(marked with a □) missing. Find the missing digits.

i

×	400 + 70 + □	47□
8		
8		□784

$8 \times 47\square = \square784$

ii

×	□0 + 7	□7
20		
+		
1		
21		1□27

$21 \times \square7 = 1\square27$

iii

×	9	9
300		
+		
□0		
+		
1		
3□1		31□9

$3\square1 \times 9 = 31\square9$

    b   How many other solutions can you find?

    c   Look at your solution in **ii**. What is special about the numbers?

    d   Look at your answer to **iii** and rearrange the digits to make a further solution to the puzzle.

A19   There is believed to be just one more solution to the puzzle using four digits. It involves two numbers between 3 and 44. Can you find them?

A20

$$A \times BC = CBA$$

$$D \times EC = CED$$

Using three digits, as in the pictures above, there are *only* two solutions. Use the following clues to try to find these two solutions:

clue 1: $100 < CBA < 200$ and $100 < CED < 200$

clue 2: $A = \frac{1}{2}$ of D

clue 3: $D - A = B - E$

B Patterns

B1   This sequence of numbers 1 1 2 3 5 8 13 ... is called the Fibonacci sequence. (Fibonacci was an Italian mathematician who first wrote about this sequence in 1202.)

Divide the second number by the first, then the third by the second and so on. Copy and complete the following:

$\frac{1}{1} = 1 \div 1 = 1$

$\frac{2}{1} = 2 \div 1 =$

$\frac{3}{2} = 3 \div 2 =$

$\frac{5}{3} = 5 \div 3 =$

$\vdots$

Continue as far as $\frac{233}{144}$. What is happening to your answers?

b   Using centimetre squared paper and a scale of 1cm to 5 units, plot the coordinates (1,1), (2,1), (3,2), (5,3) and so on. What do you notice?

B2   Eduard Lucas, a nineteenth century mathematician, used the sequence:

1   3   4   7   11   18   29   47   76   123   199   322   ...

Repeat question **B1** with this sequence. Does it behave in the same way?

B3   Make up a sequence of your own something like those in questions **B1** or **B2**. Explain your rule and investigate your sequence in the same way as you did for the sequences in the last two questions.

B4   For the following sequences, see if you can find the next two numbers and the rule for the sequence:

that is correct →

a   100   68   42   26   16   10   6   ...   **b**   4   8   12   16   20   ...

c   2   4   8   16   32   ...   **d**   384   192   96   48   ...

e   3   7   15   31   63   ...   **f**   1   4   9   16   25   ...

g   0   4   10   18   28   ...   **h**   1   5   10   16   23 ...

i   5   5   10   20   35   ...   **j**   4   7   12   19   28   ...

k   1   1   1   3   5   9   17   ...

C Squares, cubes and roots

C1 Copy this table and continue the columns until you have completed twelve lines:

Number	Number squared	Written	Value of square
1	1×1	1^2	1
2	2×2	2^2	4
3	3×3	3^2	9
12	12×12	12^2	☐

Find the key marked x^2 on your calculator. To see how it works, press **6** x^2 and see what you get.

C2 Use your calculator to find the squares of the numbers from 13 to 25. Make a list of your answers.

C3 **a** Key in the sequence: **2** x^y **3** **=** on your calculator.

(On some calculators the key may be marked y^x.)

b Now try: **3** x^y **3** **=** and
4 x^y **3** **=**

c Using your calculator, complete this table:

Number	Number cubed	Written	Value
1	$1 \times 1 \times 1$	1^3	1
2	$2 \times 2 \times 2$	2^3	8
3	$3 \times 3 \times 3$	3^3	☐
12	$12 \times 12 \times 12$	☐	☐

C4 Make a list of the cubes of the numbers from 13 to 25.

Higher powers

C5   The y^x or x^y key can be used to find higher powers of numbers

   a   Try the sequence: 5 y^x 2 = .
      Write down the answer. Can you explain what is happening?

   b   Now try: 2 y^x 5 = .
      and write down your answer

C6 **a**   Copy this table. Leave the first two names blank for now:

Name	Power	Value
	3^0	
	3^1	
Three squared	3^2	9
Three cubed	3^3	27
Three to the power 4	3^4	81
Three to the power 5	3^5	243
Three to the power 6	3^6	
Three to the power 7	3^7	
Three to the power 8	3^8	
Three to the power 9	3^9	
Three to the power 10	3^{10}	

   b   How do you get from 9 to 27 and from 27 to 81?

   c   How do you get back from 81 to 27 or from 27 to 9?

   d   To complete the table you need to go back from 9 to the number
      before, what do you think it is?
      Check on your calculator using 3 y^x 1 = .

   e   Now calculate 3 y^x 0 = .

   f   Complete the table with the names for the top two rows. These
      should be: 'Three to the power 0' and 'Three to the power 1'.

C7   Make up similar tables for powers from 0 to 10 of:

   a   2   **b**   6   **c**   10

Squares and square roots

Here is part of the table of squares you completed in question **C1**.

Number	Square
1	1
2	4
3	9
4	16
5	25
6	36

If you work backwards from the square to the original number, you are finding the **square root**. So the square root of 36 is 6.

This is written as $\sqrt{36} = 6$.
The symbol $\sqrt{}$ means square root of.

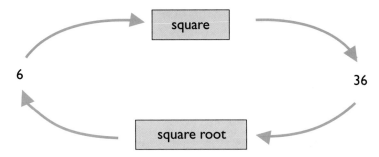

Find the $\boxed{\sqrt{x}}$ key on your calculator and then try the key sequences:
$\boxed{3}\ \boxed{6}\ \boxed{\sqrt{x}}$, $\boxed{2}\ \boxed{5}\ \boxed{\sqrt{x}}$, $\boxed{6}\ \boxed{4}\ \boxed{\sqrt{x}}$.

C8   Find the square roots of these numbers:

    a   100   **b**   144   **c**   169   **d**   225

Cubes and cube roots

Look at the table of cube numbers in question **C3**. If you work backwards in the table from a cube to the original number, you are finding the **cube root**. So the cube root of 27 is 3.

This is written as $\sqrt[3]{27} = 3$ The symbol $\sqrt[3]{}$ means cube root of.

C9   Find the cube roots of:

    a   216   **b**   125   **c**   343

C10   Find the $\boxed{\sqrt[3]{x}}$ key on your calculator. (Some calculators use $\boxed{x^y}$ or you may need to press $\boxed{\text{shift}}$ or $\boxed{\text{2ndF}}$ to make it work. If in doubt ask your teacher.) Use the key to find $\sqrt[3]{27}$ which is equal to 3.
Now calculate the cube roots of:

    a   729   **b**   1   **c**   64   **d**   1331

UNIT 4 *Directed numbers*

A Another look at the number line

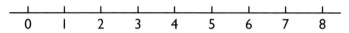

This number line has been marked at centimetre intervals. Some of the points have been labelled with **counting numbers** or **natural numbers**. you will notice that as you read these numbers from left to right, they increase in size.

A1 a If you could extend the number line to the right, what is the largest number you could record?

b When you count, do the numbers always increase in size? Find some examples to illustrate your answer.

c At the launching of a space rocket, how do scientists number the final seconds of the count down?
What moment in the firing process is labelled zero?

A2 Write down as many situations as you can which require numbers to be marked to the left of zero on the number line.

Numbers with a sign in front, like ⁺2 or ⁻3, are called **directed numbers**. The sign tells you in which direction to move away from zero. Usually positive numbers are to the right of zero on a horizontal number line and the negative numbers are to the left.

A3 Draw a number line which includes all the points from ⁻10 to ⁺10. Label it the **directed number** line. Check that you have marked and labelled twenty-one points.

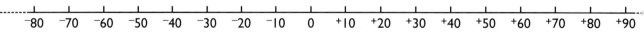

A4 Draw a number line like the one above. Use it to find the distances:

a from ⁻40 to ⁺60 **b** from ⁺80 to ⁻70 **c** from ⁻30 to ⁺90

B Games with directed numbers

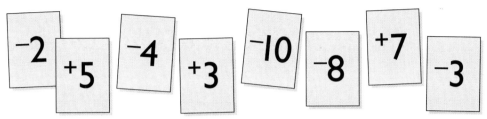

N2:3

You need to make a set of twenty-one directed number cards from ⁻10 to ⁺10 from Worksheet N2:3. You also need to prepare a set of four answer sheets like the one below:

The aim of the game is to place the cards in the correct order starting with the smallest number on the left.

You can play with four or fewer players – you can even play on your own.

Game	Answer boxes					Score
1						
2						
3						
4						
				TOTAL		

B1 Deal five cards to each player and put any remaining cards face down in the middle of the table. Each player needs an answer sheet like the one above.

Each player turns over their own top card and writes the number on the card in one of the five answer boxes for game 1.

Now each player repeats this with the second card and so on until all five boxes are filled. Then you score one point for each number that is correctly placed in order. For example:

⁻6 ⁻7 ⁺1 ⁺3 ⁺9 scores 3 (the correct order is ⁻7 ⁻6 ⁺1 ⁺3 ⁺9 and so three of the numbers are in the correct positions).

⁻4 ⁺6 0 ⁻6 ⁺8 scores 2 (only the 0 and ⁺8 are in the correct positions if you put the numbers in order).

Check the scores entered in your neighbour's answer sheet.

The winner is the player with the highest total score after four games.

B2 Repeat the game in question **B1** but this time with two players.

This time you deal ten cards to each player so you need ten answer boxes for each game.

Score as before so that a perfect score after four games would be 40 points.

C Temperatures and other measures

Here is a thermometer which can measure an unusually wide range of temperatures. The point marked A indicates the temperature at which beeswax melts (62°C).

C1 **a** Make a copy of the thermometer and mark where the following should be placed:

B the temperature at which water boils

C the temperature at which ice melts

D the temperature at which frozen food is stored ($^-$18°C)

E the highest air temperature ever recorded on Earth ($^+$58°C, Sahara Desert)

F the temperature at which carbon dioxide freezes ($^-$57°C)

G the temperature at which mercury freezes ($^-$39°C)

H the temperature on a really hot day in Britain

I the temperature at which ammonia freezes ($^-$78°C)

J a comfortable temperature in which to sit at home.

  b If you know any of the equivalent Fahrenheit temperatures, write them in brackets by the side of the Celsius ones.

C2 **a** How much colder is it when carbon dioxide freezes than when mercury freezes?

  b If 20°C is a comfortable temperature to sit and watch television, how many degrees colder is the food in the freezer?

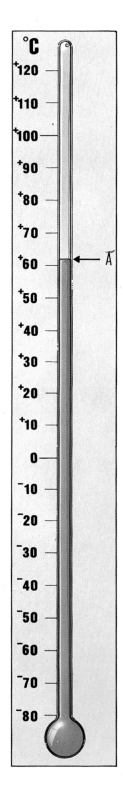

C3   In Britain the temperature on a very hot day could be 30°C and on a
very cold night it might be ⁻5°C.

WINTER

Hour	Temperature
0:00	
4:00	
8:00	
.	
.	
.	
24:00	

SUMMER

Hour	Temperature
0:00	
4:00	
8:00	
.	
.	
.	
24:00	

a   Copy and complete these tables giving what you think are suitable
temperatures at four-hour intervals.

b   What is the difference between your highest and lowest temperatures?

c   Draw a graph showing the difference between temperatures on a
winter and on a summer day.

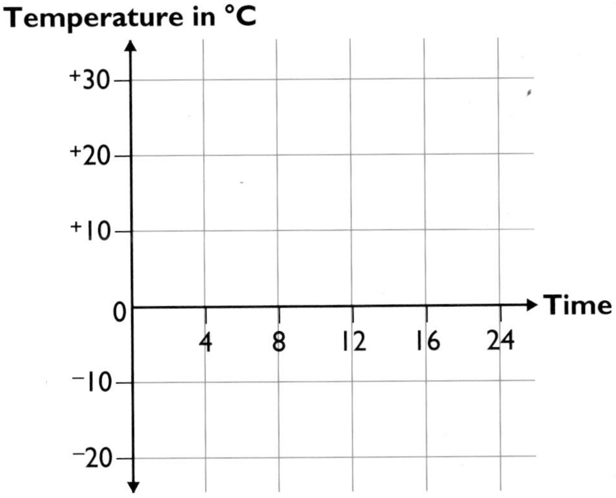

Another scale for measuring temperature is the Kelvin scale. This has a
zero temperature the same as ⁻273.15° Celsius which is known as **absolute
zero**.

C4   Draw a number line to show absolute zero together with the freezing and
boiling points of water in degrees Celsius.

Explorers have always been fascinated by the challenges of climbing high mountains and diving as deep under the oceans as possible.
The heights above sea level are measured as positive (+) distances.
The depths below sea level are measured as negative (–) distances.

C5   The highest mountain in the world is about +8754 metres high (or 29 028 feet) What is this mountain called? Find out how it got its name and who climbed it first.

C6   Here is a list of some deep ocean dives and the names of the people who made them:

Piccard 1953	–5 668 metres
Piccard and Walsch 1960	–10 916 metres
Barton 1948	–1 360 metres
Piccard 1953	–3 150 metres
Piccard 1960	–7 300 metres
Houot and Willm 1954	–4 050 metres

a   Place these dives in order.

b   What is the difference (in metres) between the first and last dives in the list?

c   Which two dives had the least difference between them? How many metres was it?

C7   What is the difference in metres between the height of the world's highest mountain (in question **C5**) and the dive by Piccard and Walsh (in question **C6**)?

C8   Design a number line to include all the heights and depths in questions **C5** and **C6**.

C9   Add to the line the heights of two other mountains of your choice.

C10 Hannas Keller from Switzerland has made dives of 302 metres just wearing a diving suit. Add his dive to your number line.

D More games with directed numbers

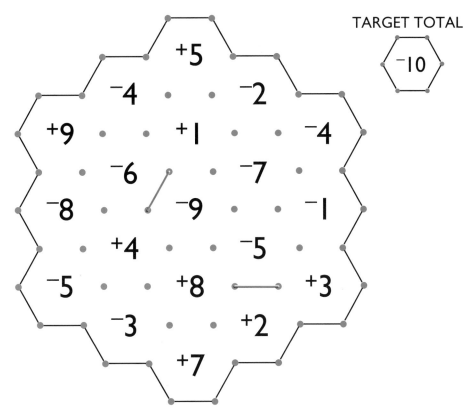

TARGET TOTAL

⁻10

This game, called *Track and Trap*, is for two players.

You will need two different coloured pens and a grid like the one above from Worksheet N2:4.

The aim of the game is to complete, and in that way capture hexagons so that the total of the numbers inside each player's hexagons is as close as possible to ⁻10.

Take it in turns to draw in two lines connecting two adjacent points. (As shown in the diagram above.) The lines do not need to be connected or part of the same small hexagon. When you complete a hexagon, put your initials in it to show that you have captured it. When you complete a hexagon you can also draw one extra line.

When all the hexagons have been captured each player adds up the totals in their hexagons and the winner is the player who has a total nearest to ⁻10.

Here is a game in progress between Caroline and Jignna.

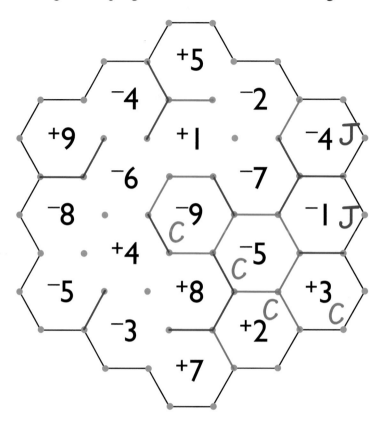

D1   Caroline has prepared a directed number line to help her work out her score. What is Caroline's total score so far?

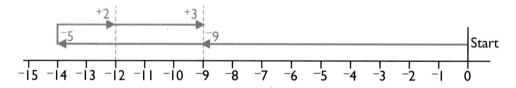

D2   What is Jignna's score so far?

Play *Track and Trap* using different target numbers.

E Operation hexagon (addition)

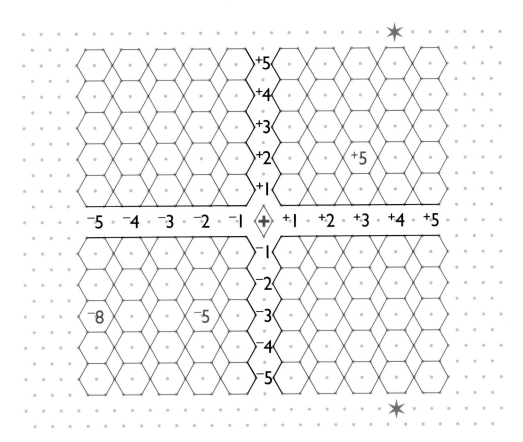

In the grid above, which works like the Cayley tables you met in Unit 3, you can put in the results of adding numbers. For example:

$$^+3 + {}^+2 = {}^+5 \qquad\qquad {}^-2 + {}^-3 = {}^-5 \qquad\qquad {}^-5 + {}^-3 = {}^-8$$

N2:5

E1 On a copy of the grid (either make your own or use Worksheet N2:5) fill in all the missing numbers in the hexagons. Check some of your answers on a calculator.

E2 Lightly shade all the positive numbers in one colour and all the negative ones in another. Make a note of any patterns you notice.

E3 Look carefully at the numbers in the column between the two red stars. What do you notice? Can you explain what you see?

F The cross-country event

At an end-of-season charity event it is the custom for four local clubs each to enter a team of ten runners in a cross-country run.

The teams wear blue (B), green (G), red (R) and yellow (Y) shirts.

Here is the finishing order:

1 Y	2 G	3 B	4 G	5 R	6 R	7 R	8 B	9 Y	10 Y
11 G	12 B	13 R	14 Y	15 G	16 G	17 B	18 G	19 Y	20 R
21 B	22 Y	23 Y	24 G	25 R	26 G	27 Y	28 B	29 B	30 G
31 R	32 B	33 G	34 Y	35 Y	36 B	37 R	38 R	39 B	40 R

Each member of the team scores points depending on their position in the finishing order. The winner receives 20 points, the second runner 19, the third 18 and so on.

F1   Which runner gains no points for his or her team?

F2   What is the score of the last runner?

F3   Which team had the highest score? What was the score?

F4   Find the scores of all the teams if the last two runners in each team are not counted.

G Operation hexagon (subtraction)

On page 38 you completed a hexagon grid for addition.

N2:6

G1   Now either copy the grid opposite or use Worksheet N2:6. Complete the grid using the operation of *subtraction*. Make sure you always start with a number on the horizontal line. Check your answers on a calculator.

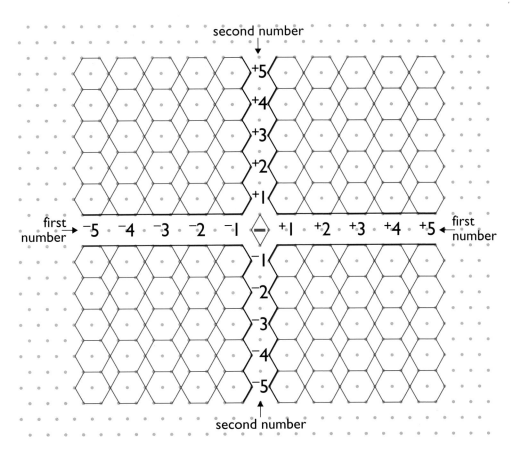

G2 Lightly shade all the negative numbers in one colour and the positive ones in another. What do you notice?

G3 Using the directed number line you prepared in **A3** look at ⁻2 – ⁻3 Can you explain what is happening? What happens with a double negative? (For example, what does 'I can't not do my homework' really mean?)

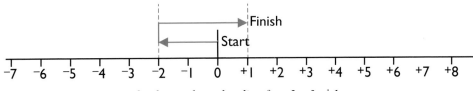

Using the directed number line for ⁻2–⁻3=⁺1

G4 Do these calculations using your directed number line from question **A3** and then check your answers with a calculator:

a	⁺3 – ⁺2	**b**	⁻3 – ⁺2	
c	⁺3 – ⁻2	**d**	⁻3 – ⁻2	
e	⁺8 – ⁺5	**f**	⁻8 – ⁺5	
g	⁺8 – ⁻5	**h**	⁻8 – ⁻5	
i	⁻2 – ⁻1	**j**	⁺5 – ⁻3	
k	⁺4 – ⁻4	**l**	⁻5 – ⁻5	

UNIT 5 *Computer programs and sequences*

A Triangular numbers

Look at this sequence of numbers: 1   3   6   10   15   ...
They are called **triangular** numbers

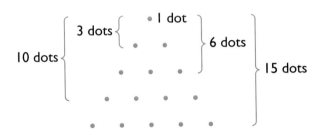

A1 Why do you think the numbers above have the name triangular numbers?
(If you have not seen them before, try making a pattern of dots for each
number.) Write down the first ten triangular numbers.

A2 What does the following computer program do?
Run it and check for yourself using:

a N = 5   **b** N = 10   **c** N = 20

I wonder how
I can find the nth
trianglar number?

```
10 REM: TRIANGULAR NUMBERS
20 INPUT N
30 LET T = 0
40 FOR C = 1 TO N
50 LET T = T + C
60 PRINT T
70 NEXT C
```

Some notes on the program:

1. Use a REM (remark) so you remember what the program is about.
2. N identifies the length of the list you require.
3. C is a counter which counts from 1 to N.
4. T gives the actual triangular number each time.
5. Each time you use the program you must select the INPUT, N.

A3 Imagine you piled cans as shown.

You would be making a pyramid of triangular numbers. Try to write
down a sequence of the first ten **triangular pyramid** numbers.

A4 Look at this program and write down what you think it will do.

```
10 REM: TRIANGULAR PYRAMID NUMBERS
20 LET D = 0
30 INPUT A
40 LET D = D + A
50 PRINT D
60 GOTO 30
```

Run the program putting in the first ten triangular numbers as inputs in
turn. Check the output against the triangular pyramid numbers which
you listed in question **A3**.

Some notes on the program:

1. For A, you need to input the triangular numbers one by one.
2. D adds the triangular numbers together as if you were counting cans
    on removal from a pyramidal pile starting at the top.

B Square numbers and higher powers

B1 What is a **square** number? (Make a pattern of dots for each number if you need to.)
Write down a list of the first ten square numbers.
Write a computer program to give you a list of square numbers. Run it to check that it works.

BASIC

B2 Here are some programs. Explain what they do and compare them with your program in question **B1**.
(The REM commands are incomplete. How should they be completed?)

a
```
10 REM
20 FOR NUMBER = 1 TO 13
30 PRINT NUMBER * NUMBER
40 NEXT NUMBER
50 END
```

b
```
10 REM
20 FOR A = 1 TO 13
30 LET S = A * A
40 PRINT A; "*";A;"=";S
50 NEXT A
```

c
```
10 REM
20 FOR N = 1 TO 13
30 LET S = N^2
40 PRINT N,S
50 NEXT N
```

Run the three programs to check that you were correct about what you thought should happen.

B3 Write a simple program to find the square of *any* number (not just whole numbers) and use your program to find the squares of:

a 1.2 **b** 3.9 **c** 8.1 **d** 11.04 **e** 2.22

You can check that your program is working by re-doing the calculations on your calculator.

B4 What does this program do? (The REM command has again been left blank for you to complete later.)

```
10 REM
20 FOR N = 1 TO 13
30 LET S = N*N*N
40 PRINT N,S
50 NEXT N
```

Run the program and see what happens.
Now change command 30 to '30 LET S = N^3' and run the new program. Keep a note of your results.

B5 Write a program to find the cubes of all the numbers from 20 to 30. Test by running it.

B6 Modify one of the commands in question **B4** to print the **fourth powers** of the numbers from 1 to 13. Run the program and write down the results.

B7 Write a program to find powers of numbers that are not whole numbers and test it by finding:

    a 2.3^4 **b** 5.87^3 **c** 54.67^5 **d** 0.89^3

Check the answers with a calculator.

B8

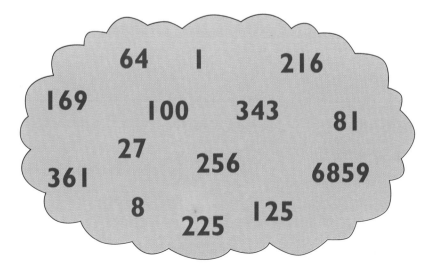

    a Which of the numbers above are *square* numbers?

    b Which are *cube* numbers?

    c Which are *both* square and cube numbers?

C Other sequences

C1 Question **A4** described how to write a program to give triangular pyramid numbers. Write a similar program to find **square pyramid** numbers based on square numbers like the ones below.

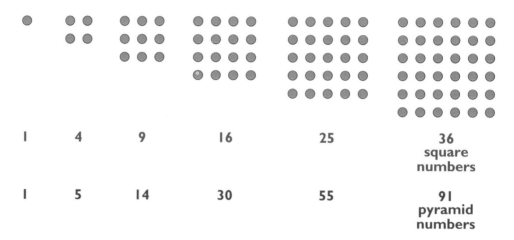

1	4	9	16	25	36 square numbers
1	5	14	30	55	91 pyramid numbers

C2 Are there any triangular numbers that are also square numbers?
Work out what this program will do:

```
10 REM
20 INPUT N
30 LET T = 0
40 FOR C = 1 TO N
50 LET T = T + C
60 IF SQR(T) = INT(SQR(T)) THEN PRINT T
70 NEXT C
```

See what happens when you run the program with:

a N = 100   **b** N = 1000

Explain your results.

You may not be familiar with the instructions SQR and INT:

SQR finds the square root of a number.

INT converts any number which is not already a whole number to the nearest whole number below; for example, 5.21 would become 5. (That is it chops off all the digits to the right of any decimal point.)

D Square roots

BASIC

D1 What does this program do?

```
10 REM
20 FOR B = 1 TO 10
30 LET A = SQR(B)
40 PRINT "SQUARE ROOT OF "; B; "IS ";A
50 NEXT B
```

Run the program and keep a note of your results.

D2 Working with a friend, see how close you can get to the square root of a number by guessing.

For example, start with 720.

1st guess:	square root is 20	20^2	= 400	too low
2nd guess:	square root is 29	29^2	= 841	too high
3rd guess:	square root is 27	27^2	= 729	too high but closer
4th guess:	square root is 26	26^2	= 676	too low
5th guess:	square root is 26.8	26.8^2	= 718.24	too low but closer
6th guess:	square root is 26.84	26.84^2	= 720.38	too high but closer

and so on.

D3 Copy and complete this program.

```
10 REM
20 INPUT N
30 LET B = _____ - _____
40 PRINT _____ , _____
50 GO TO 20
```

where N = guessed square root of 60 and B tells you how close your guess is to the exact square root. Your second input will be your second guess and so on.

Try the program for square roots of numbers other than 60.

E More patterns

BASIC

E1 What sequence does this program produce?

```
10 REM: GUESS THE SEQUENCE
20 LET M = 3
30 LET N = 1
40 PRINT M
50 LET M = M + 3
60 LET N = N + 1
70 IF N > 20 THEN STOP
80 GO TO 30
```

Run the program and keep a note of the output.
Write some programs of your own to give similar sequences and run them to check that they work.

E2 What does this program do?

```
10 REM
20 FOR I = 1 TO 10
30 E = I * 3 + 2
40 PRINT I, E
50 NEXT I
```

I stands for **input** and E for **output**.
Run the program and keep a list of inputs and outputs. Write down what you think the program does.

E3 Write programs to give:

a A sequence given by I * 4 - 2 where I goes from 1 to 10.

b A sequence given by 12 - I where I goes from 1 to 12.

E4 Write a program to give a sequence of your own choice.

E5   Try these programs and see if you can decide what is happening:

a
```
10 REM
20 FOR NUMBER = 2 TO 22
30 PRINT 4 * NUMBER
40 NEXT NUMBER
50 END
```

b
```
10 REM
20 PRINT "What number is P?"
30 INPUT P
40 PRINT "What number is Q?"
50 INPUT Q
60 PRINT 2 * P * P + Q
```

Put in six different values for P and Q and record your results in a table.

E6   Try to work out what this program does and then run it to see if you were right.
```
10 REM
20 FOR N = 1 TO 10
30 T = (N + 1)/N
40 PRINT T
50 NEXT N
60 END
```

E7   Run the program in question **E6** with line 30 changed to:

a   T = N/(N + 1)   **b**   T = 4/N

c   T = (N + 1)/2*N   **d**   T = 1 - N

Write down your results and explain what is happening each time.

E8   Look back at the Fibonacci sequence in question **B1** on page 27. Now run this program and describe what it does:

```
10 REM: FIBONACCI SEQUENCE
20 INPUT N
30 LET X = 1
40 LET Y = 1
50 FOR C = 1 TO N
60 PRINT X
70 LET Z = X + Y
80 LET X = Y
90 LET Y = Z
100 NEXT C
110 END
```

Try with different input values for N.
What does the program give you?

E9   Look at these two sequences:

a 1 1 2 4 7 13 24 44 81 ...

b 1 1 2 4 8 15 29 56 108 ...

Can you see a pattern? Write down the next two terms in each sequence. Write computer programs to give you these sequences and use the programs to print the first 20 terms in each case.

E10 **Extension work** A fast growing bean plant doubles its height every day. Today (day 1) it is 0.5 cm high.

   a Write a computer program to print the height of the plant for days 1 to 25.

   b How high will the plant be on day 100?

F Spreadsheets and sequences

You could use a **spreadsheet** to help you explore sequences.

A computer program can produce a spreadsheet which appears on your screen as a grid with rows numbered 1, 2, 3, 4, 5 … and columns lettered A, B, C, D, E …

The spaces are called **cells** and they are identified by the column and row they appear in. For example, B2 is the cell in column B and row 2.

A big advantage of spreadsheets is that they will carry out calculations for you. The required formula (instruction to the computer) is put into the cell of one column and can be automatically copied into each cell below. The spreadsheet does not display the formula on the screen but shows you the calculated values.

	A	B	C
1			
2			
3			
4			
5			
6			
7			

F1 Set up a spreadsheet for the Fibonacci sequence.

Notes to help you:

1. Use rows 1 to 25 and columns A and B.
2. Rows 1 and 2 are for headings, row 3 is blank as a separator.
3. Enter values '1' in cells A4 and A5, these are the first two terms.
4. Put the formula A4 + A5 into cell A6 and copy it down the rest of column A.
5. Start in cell B5 with the formula A5/A4 and copy this down the rest of column B.

When your spreadsheet is complete, compare your results with those obtained on page 27.

I think he said get a spreadsheet not spread a groundsheet!

51

UNIT 6 *Multiplication and division*

A Multiplying directed numbers

A1 Copy and complete these Cayley tables. (Hint: look back at Unit 3, if you need to, to remind you how to use Cayley tables.)

a

×	+5	+7	(+8)
+10			
−3			
(+7)			+56

b

×		(+8)
+10		
−3		
(+7)	+56	

c

×	+10	−2	(+8)
(+7)			+56

A2 From your tables in question **A1**, give the answers to these multiplications:

a −3 × +3 **b** +8 × −3 **c** +7 × −2

What can you say about a plus (+) multiplied by a minus (−)?

A3 Copy and complete these tables.

a

×	+10	−2	(+8)
+10			
−3		✳	
(+7)			+56

b

×	+9	−1	(+8)
+9			
−2		✳	
(+7)			+56

c

×	+11	−3	(+8)
+11			
−4		✳	
(+7)			+56

What do you notice about the boxes labelled ✳ ?

A4 From your tables in question **A3**, give answers to these multiplications:

a −3 × −2 **b** −2 × −1 **c** −4 × −3

What can you say about a minus (−) multiplied by a minus (−)?

N2:7

A5 Complete the multiplication grid on Worksheet N2:7, shown on the next page. Lightly shade negative numbers in one colour and positive numbers in another. Comment on any pattern you notice.

A6 Find two places in your grid where you have +12. What are the multiplications which give you these answers?

A7 Now find two places where you have −12 and write down the multiplications giving these answers.

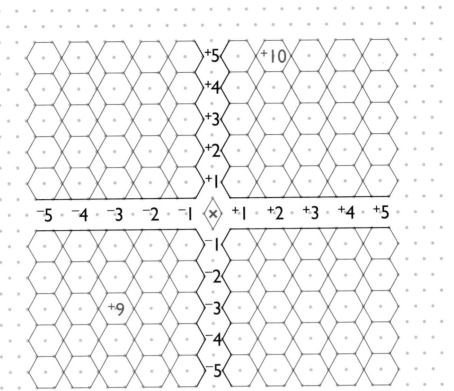

A8   Calculate these multiplications:

    a $^+4 \times {^+}3$ **b** $^+4 \times {^-}3$ **c** $^-4 \times {^+}3$ **d** $^-4 \times {^-}3$

    e $^+12 \times {^+}5$ **f** $^+12 \times {^-}5$ **g** $^-12 \times {^+}5$ **h** $^-12 \times {^-}5$

    Check your answers on a calculator.

    A multiplication sum can also be written as a division sum.
    For example: $5 \times 3 = 15$ could be written as $15 \div 3 = 5$.

A9   Using this idea and your multiplication grid, calculate these divisions:

    a $^+4 \div {^+}2$ **b** $^+4 \div {^-}2$ **c** $^-4 \div {^+}2$ **d** $^-4 \div {^-}2$

    e $^+12 \div {^+}3$ **f** $^+12 \div {^-}3$ **g** $^-12 \div {^+}3$ **h** $^-12 \div {^-}3$

    Can you make a statement about what happens when you divide directed
    numbers? Check your answers on a calculator.

A10 Make up some calculations involving directed numbers which give these answers:

    a $^+6$ **b** $^-8$ **c** $^+3$ **d** $^-3$ **e** $^+10$ **f** $^-5$ **g** 0

    Make up three questions for each answer and check them on your calculator.

B Division and multiplication

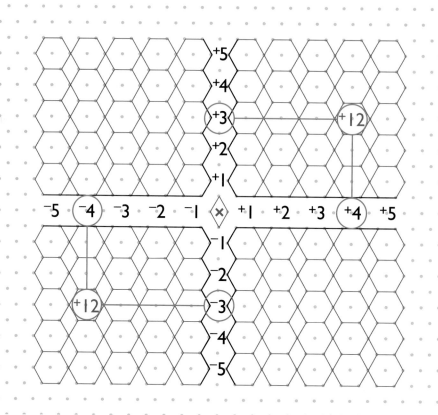

This multiplication grid shows that: $^+3 \times ^+4 = ^+12$ and $^-3 \times ^-4 = ^+12$
and also: $^+12 \div ^+4 = ^+3$ and $^+12 \div ^-4 = ^-3$

Division is the inverse operation of multiplication.

B1 Without using a calculator, find:
391 ÷ 17
Show all your working.

B2 Find as many different ways as possible to do the calculation in question
B1 and write them down. For example:

10 lots of 17 =	170	
10 lots of 17 =	170	
2 lots of 17 =	34	
1 lot of 17 =	17	
23 lots of 17 =	391	

```
  391
 -170
  221
 -170
   51
  -34
   17
```

So: 391 ÷ 17 = 23

Using a Cayley table:

×	20	⁻3	17
20	400	⁻60	340
2	40	⁻6	34
1	20	⁻3	17
Answer 23			391

So: $391 \div 17 = 23$

B3 Compare your methods with those of a friend and decide which method you think is best. Explain your choice.

B4 Use any method you like to find the following without using a calculator:

a	$576 \div 9$	**b**	$696 \div 12$	**c**	$775 \div 25$	**d**	$612 \div 18$
e	$851 \div 23$	**f**	$891 \div 27$	**g**	$874 \div 19$	**h**	$999 \div 37$
i	$2394 \div 38$	**j**	$2548 \div 52$	**k**	$1943 \div 67$	**l**	$4305 \div 35$

m $56\,088 \div 123$

Check your answers with a calculator.

B5 What is $360 \div 30$? Try to work it out in your head.

B6 Do the calculation in question **B5** in several different ways. Write each way down. For example:

$$3 \times 12 = 36 \qquad \text{or} \qquad 360 = 36 \text{ tens}$$
$$30 \times 12 = 36 \times 10 \qquad\qquad 30 = 3 \text{ tens}$$
$$= 360 \qquad\qquad \text{there are 12 lots of 3 tens}$$
$$\text{in 36 tens and so}$$
$$\text{So: } 360 \div 30 = 12 \qquad\qquad 360 \div 30 = 12$$

B7 Explain which of your methods you think is best and why.

B8 Write down a rule for dividing multiples of ten by ten and then find these without using a calculator:

a	$180 \div 9$	**b**	$2400 \div 120$	**c**	$1000 \div 50$	**d**	$480 \div 24$
e	$960 \div 20$	**f**	$960 \div 40$	**g**	$2000 \div 40$	**h**	$2010 \div 30$
i	$1700 \div 50$	**j**	$17\,400 \div 60$				

Check your answers with a calculator.

C **Remainders**

C1   A group of 256 pupils went on a day trip to London. They were accompanied by 22 adults. The only coaches available were 52 seaters. How many coaches were needed?

C2   Suppose the organizer of the trip in question **C1** had a choice of 45-seater and 52-seater coaches. Would the same number of coaches still be needed? Explain your answer.

In the following questions give answers which relate to the problem posed and are based on common sense. Do not use a calculator.

C3   A class of 29 pupils was given a box of chocolates. If the box contained 250 chocolates, how could they be distributed so that the box was completely empty by the end of the day?

C4   Three people are playing a game of cards using a pack which contains 52 cards. How would you arrange the dealing of the cards so that no-one felt they were at a disadvantage?

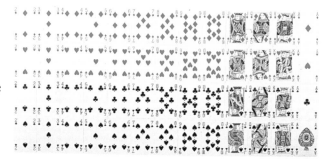

C5 On sports day 75 girls wanted to run in the 400 metres. Only six girls could take part in any heat.

   a How many preliminary heats were needed? Explain how you get your answer. Would all the runners feel that the heats had been fairly arranged?

   b In the final there are to be six runners. Plan the organization of the heats leading up to the final. (You may need quarter-finals or semi-finals.)

C6 George's grandfather died leaving £68 000 to be shared equally between George and his ten cousins.

   a How much did each receive?

   b Explain what might have happened to the remainder once the money had been shared.

C7 A normal year has 365 days and 52 weeks.
But $7 \times 52 = 364$
Can you explain this?

D **Recurring decimals**

Sharing (or division) frequently involves an answer that includes fractions or decimals. All remainders can be expressed as fractions which in turn can be expressed as decimal fractions.

If the denominator is a factor of a power of 10, then the fraction will terminate. For example:

$\frac{1}{4}$ = 0.25   (4 is a factor of 10^2)

$\frac{1}{16}$ = 0.0625   (16 is a factor of 10^4)

D1

Use your calculator to check that the fractions in the picture above do become terminating decimals.

If the denominator does not divide exactly into a power of 10, then the fraction recurs. For example:

$\frac{17}{99}$ = 0.171717 ...

D2

Use your calculator to check that the fractions in the picture above become recurring decimals.

D3   Write these fractions as recurring decimals using dot notation.
(Dot notation for recurring decimals was introduced on page 9.)

a $\frac{1}{3}$ **b** $\frac{4}{11}$ **c** $\frac{6}{7}$ **d** $\frac{2}{3}$ **e** $\frac{1}{9}$ **f** $\frac{5}{9}$

D4   Here are conversions of $\frac{6}{7}$ on four different calculators:

Did you get any of these in question **D3**. Which one is correct?

Here is a method for converting a fraction ($\frac{3}{8}$) to a decimal fraction:

Units		$\frac{1}{10}$	$\frac{1}{100}$	$\frac{1}{1000}$
0	.	3	7	5
8) 3	.	0	0	0

This is called **long division**. You change the 3 Units to 30 tenths. Divide $\frac{30}{10}$ by 8 to give $\frac{3}{10}$ with remainder 6. You then change these 6 tenths to $\frac{60}{100}$ and divide by 8 to get $\frac{7}{100}$ with remainder 4.
Finally you change the $\frac{4}{100}$ to $\frac{40}{1000}$ and divide by 8 to get $\frac{5}{1000}$ exactly.

So: $\frac{3}{8}$ = 0.375

If you try this method on $\frac{6}{7}$ you get:

```
     0 . 8 5 7 1 4 2 8 5 7 1 4 2 8
 7 ) 6 . 0 0 0 0 0 0 0 0 0 0 0 0 0
```

Check through the calculation which gives:
$\frac{6}{7}$ = 0.857142857142 … = 0.$\dot{8}$5714$\dot{2}$

and shows us that $\frac{6}{7}$ gives a recurring decimal.

D5   Use this method to convert the other members of the sevenths family to decimals.

D6   Use the method to convert these fractions to decimals:

   a $\frac{2}{3}$ **b** $\frac{4}{9}$ **c** $\frac{5}{11}$ **d** $\frac{8}{11}$ **e** $\frac{5}{13}$ **f** $\frac{2}{17}$ **g** $\frac{3}{19}$

D7   Convert $\frac{4}{9}$ and $\frac{5}{9}$ to decimals. Add your answers together without using a calculator.

E Looking for patterns

E1   Investigate the recurring patterns of the sevenths, thirteenths, seventeenths and nineteenths families of fractions.

    a   How many digits are there in each recurring pattern?

    b   Predict the number of digits which recur for $\frac{1}{23}$.

    c   Which is the next family which will have a similar property to the twenty-thirds family?

E2   Rewrite the decimal fractions for the ninths fraction family both with and without the recurring dots.
Which ones have you met elsewhere?

E3   Answer question **E2** for the elevenths family. What do you notice?

E4   Look at the recurring pattern for one seventh.

    a   What do you notice?

    b   Put the six numbers in the sevenths pattern around the edge of a circle.

    c   What happens if you do the same for other members of the sevenths family?

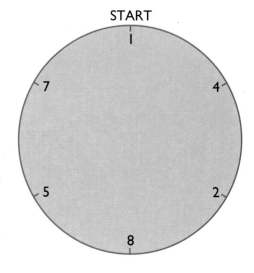

E5 **a** Find as many recurring decimals as you can which have the number three as one of the digits involved.

b Multiply together the recurring decimals for $\frac{1}{3}$ and $\frac{1}{9}$. What answer do you get?

c If you multiply two recurring decimals will you always get a recurring decimal as your answer? Explain your conclusion.

E6

Find out what numbers other people think are lucky or unlucky.
Try to discover why these numbers are regarded as lucky or unlucky.

UNIT 7 *Hundredths and percentages*

A The hundredth in everyday life

One of the most frequently used fractions is the **hundredth**.

A1   "The sprinter won the race by one hundredth of a second."
Write down three other situations in everyday life where you might come across hundredths and in each case indicate clearly which part of your example involves their use. Compare notes and discuss your situations with a friend.

> Remember: the hundredth in its decimal form is **0.01**

A2   Copy this table, leaving space for several more lines:

	←		British currency			→			Remainder	
M	HTh	TTh	Th	H	T	U	$\frac{1}{10}$	$\frac{1}{100}$	$\frac{1}{1000}$	$\frac{1}{10000}$
				1	2	3	4	5		

a   Explain why the $\frac{1}{1000}$ column cannot be included under the British currency heading and state, in words, the sum of money already entered.

b   Find examples of money used in other countries. How do they compare with the British system? Do any use thousandths?

A3   Mrs Evans wanted 3.7 metres of material at £8.59 per metre to make a blouse.

a   Use your calculator to find out how much her blouse material cost.

b   She also decided to buy some matching material to make a skirt and bought 2.9 metres at £9.32 per metre. Calculate how much her skirt material cost.

A4 **a** Put the amount you calculated for the cost of the blouse material in question **A3a** in the table you prepared in question **A2**.

  b Put the cost of the skirt material in the table as well.

  c What do you notice?

  d Can you suggest what would be a fair amount for Mrs Evans to pay the shopkeeper for the materials?

A5 Mrs Evans also bought 1.5 metres of silk to make a tie and scarf.
The silk cost £15.99 per metre.

  a Put the cost of the silk in your table in question **A2**.

  b Use the same rule you used to answer question **A4d** to work out how much Mrs Evans should pay for the silk.

  c Explain the rule you used in part **b** above.

Aiming for accuracy

You will need your number line from Unit 2 and some 1mm graph paper.

The smallest coin in use in Great Britain is 1p or £$\frac{1}{100}$.
Your calculations of the cost of materials in questions
A3 – A5 should have given you the following values:

The blouse material cost   £31.78 | 3

The skirt material cost   £27.02 | 8

The silk cost   £23.98 | 5

Suggest what could be done about the £$\frac{3}{1000}$, £$\frac{8}{1000}$ and £$\frac{5}{1000}$ to the right of the red lines above.

A6 Look at the number line you made in Unit 2. Prepare an enlargement of the section from $\frac{78}{100}$ to $\frac{79}{100}$ on millimetre paper as shown here:

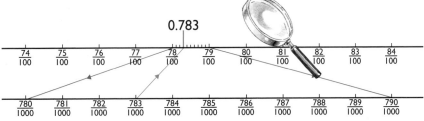

  a Is 0.783 closer to 0.780 ($\frac{78}{100}$) or 0.790 ($\frac{79}{100}$)?

  b Use the number line to decide what amount should be charged for Mrs Evans' blouse material.

A7   Using a magnified number line like the one you prepared in question **A6**, find out what the charge should be for the skirt material.

When the digit in the thousandths column is a 5 then the number is exactly half way between the two lots of hundredths. When this happens, we approximate to the number *above* rather than to the number below.

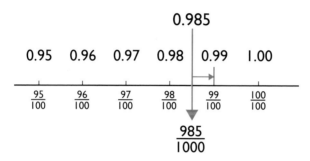

So: 0.985 gives 0.99 corrected to the **nearest hundredth**

and   0.985 gives 0.99 correct to **two decimal places**.

A8   **a**   What was Mrs Evans' total bill for the blouse material, the skirt material and the silk?

b   Does it make any difference whether each individual item is corrected to the nearest penny or just the total bill is corrected?
Explain your answer.

B Correcting to two decimal places

B1 Correct these decimals to *two* decimal places (i.e. to the nearest hundredth):

    a 0.768   **b** 0.381   **c** 0.497   **d** 0.565   **e** 0.989   **f** 0.238
    g 0.012   **h** 0.095   **i** 3.255   **j** 4.967   **k** 5.999   **l** 0.006

B2 Four different calculators gave these answers when working out $\frac{6}{7}$:

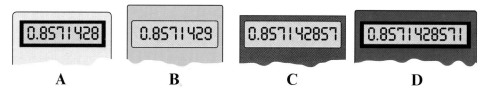

    A   **B**   **C**   **D**

    a $\frac{6}{7} = 0.8\square$ correct to two decimal places.
       Copy and complete the statement

    b Can you explain why calculators **A** and **B** each give seven places of decimals but are not the same?

    c How many decimal places must be involved before
       (i) calculators **A** and **B**   (ii) calculators **C** and **D**
       give different answers? Give reasons for your answer.

B3 Copy and complete this table for recurring decimals:

Fraction	Decimal fraction	Corrected to two decimal places
$\frac{1}{9}$		
$\frac{2}{9}$		
$\frac{1}{3}$		
$\frac{6}{9}$		
$\frac{7}{9}$		
$\frac{2}{11}$		
$\frac{8}{11}$		
$\frac{9}{11}$		
$\frac{9}{22}$		
$\frac{10}{11}$		
$\frac{43}{44}$		
$\frac{98}{99}$		

Some calculators have a key which will automatically correct an answer to a given number of decimal places. Check to see if your calculator can do this.

C Changing fractions into percentages

Hundredths

- The British money system divides £1 into a *hundred* parts.

- Often the most useful fraction of a metre is the centimetre, and measurements like height are usually given to the nearest *hundredth* of a metre. For example, David is 1.54 metres tall.

- Ingredients in medicines often require minute weights given in one *hundredth* parts of a milligram. For example, vitamin yeast tablets contain:

  – thiamin (vitamin B1)   0.15 mg per tablet

  – riboflavin (vitamin B2)   0.22 mg per tablet

- Details on food packets about the nutritional contents of food are often given per *hundred* grams. For example, a batter mix may contain:

  – protein   5.0 g per 100 g

  – carbohydrate   23.0 g per 100 g

In all these examples the measures are expressed in *hundredth* parts. One hundredth part of a measure is called **one per cent** (from the Latin 'per centum' meaning 'by the hundred').

> **A percentage always has the denominator of 100.**
> **1 out of 100 = $\frac{1}{100}$ = 1 per cent.**
> **1 per cent can also be written as 1%.**

C1 **a** On the number line you prepared in Unit 2, fill in the percentages as shown below.

0%	1%	2%	3%	4%					
0	0.01	0.02	0.03	0.04	0.05	0.06	0.07	0.08	0.09
0	$\frac{1}{100}$	$\frac{2}{100}$	$\frac{3}{100}$	$\frac{4}{100}$	$\frac{5}{100}$	$\frac{6}{100}$	$\frac{7}{100}$	$\frac{8}{100}$	$\frac{9}{100}$
		$\frac{1}{50}$		$\frac{2}{50}$		$\frac{3}{50}$		$\frac{4}{50}$	
		$\frac{1}{25}$						$\frac{2}{25}$	

b How many per cent did you record for 1?

c Which of the fraction families do not accurately become percentages?

d Is **c** true for *all* members of a family? (Consider the eighths family. Give a reason why some of the eighths family can be converted to whole percentages and others can not.)

Other fractions

Consider the fraction $\frac{3}{4}$.

On your number line there are many fractions which are equivalent to $\frac{3}{4}$. One of these is $\frac{75}{100}$.

So: $\frac{3}{4} = 75\%$

C2 Use your number line to find the percentage equivalents of these fractions:

a $\frac{3}{20}$ **b** $\frac{4}{50}$ **c** $\frac{12}{25}$ **d** $\frac{7}{10}$ **e** $\frac{4}{5}$ **f** $\frac{17}{20}$

g $\frac{49}{50}$ **h** $\frac{24}{25}$ **i** $\frac{9}{10}$ **j** $\frac{3}{50}$ **k** $\frac{19}{20}$ **l** $\frac{6}{8}$

C3 Look at this example:

Check this on your number line.

In the same way convert these fractions to percentages:

a $\frac{3}{10}$ **b** $\frac{4}{25}$ **c** $\frac{7}{20}$ **d** $\frac{9}{25}$ **e** $\frac{11}{50}$ **f** $\frac{17}{25}$

g $\frac{23}{25}$ **h** $\frac{41}{50}$ **i** $\frac{3}{5}$ **j** $\frac{31}{50}$ **k** $\frac{2}{8}$ **l** $\frac{21}{25}$

C4

> **hundred**
> cent
> honderd
> cento   cien   ekató

a Which languages do these words come from?

b Find as many other ways of writing a 'hundred' in different languages as you can.

N2:8

metre rule
plastic straws

C5   *Spot the Place*

Make a set of *Spot the Place* cards from Worksheet N2:8.

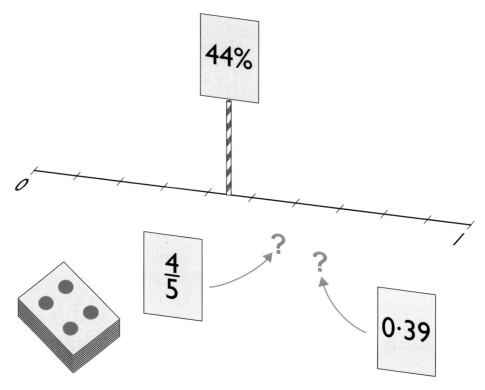

Make a number line just over 1 metre in length and mark 0 and 1 exactly
1 metre apart, as shown above.

Mark the line at 10 cm intervals but do not label these marks.

Shuffle the *Spot the Place* cards.

Turn over the top card and place it in its correct position on the number
line using a straw to mark the *exact* spot on the line. Continue until you
have used ten cards and then make a record of your results on your
number line.

Repeat for another set of ten cards.

Remember always to record your results.

C6 Without using either your number line or a calculator, copy and complete the following inserting the correct sign:
$<$ $>$ or $=$
in each of the boxes:

a 44% ☐ $\frac{1}{2}$ ☐ 0.56 b 52% ☐ $\frac{2}{5}$ c $\frac{3}{10}$ ☐ 33%

d $\frac{30}{100}$ ☐ $\frac{3}{10}$ ☐ 0.3 e $\frac{7}{100}$ ☐ $\frac{1}{20}$ ☐ 0.02

f 55% ☐ 0.54 ☐ $\frac{2}{5}$ g 3% ☐ 0.3 h $\frac{2}{8}$ ☐ 16%

i $\frac{3}{25}$ ☐ 11% ☐ 0.09 j 0.24 ☐ $\frac{1}{4}$ ☐ 26%

k $\frac{6}{8}$ ☐ 74% ☐ $\frac{17}{20}$ l 0.33 ☐ $\frac{2}{3}$ ☐ 34%

m $\frac{66}{100}$ ☐ $\frac{2}{3}$ ☐ 67% n 37% ☐ $\frac{3}{8}$ ☐ 0.38

Now check you answers on your number line.

C7 Write down the percentages for the following:

a $\frac{1}{2}$ b 1 c $1\frac{1}{2}$ d $\frac{1}{4}$ e $1\frac{1}{4}$

f $\frac{1}{5}$ g $1\frac{1}{5}$ h 2 i $2\frac{1}{2}$ j 10

You may have found some of the parts of question **C7** difficult to check on your number line. For example, writing the percentage for the number 2.

Remember that 2 can be written $\frac{2}{1}$ and so you have to work out:
$$2 = \frac{2}{1} = \frac{☐}{100}$$

So: $2 = \frac{200}{100} = 200\%$

Similarly: $1\frac{1}{4} = \frac{5}{4} = \frac{125}{100} = 125\%$

C8 Look at this table:

Fraction	Decimal fraction				Percentage
	Units	$\frac{1}{10}$	$\frac{1}{100}$	$\frac{1}{1000}$	
$\frac{36}{100}$	0	3	6		36%
$\frac{17}{25}$	0	6	8		68%
$\frac{19}{20}$	0	9	5		95%

a Check with your calculator that the fraction conversions to decimals are correct.

b Use your number line to check the accuracy of the percentages.

c What do you notice? Give a reason for your answer.

C9 Draw a table like the one in question **C8** and fill it in for the following fractions:

a $\frac{4}{5}$ b $\frac{13}{25}$ c $\frac{17}{20}$ d $\frac{19}{25}$ e $\frac{23}{50}$

f $\frac{3}{10}$ g $\frac{50}{25}$ h $\frac{5}{8}$ i $\frac{1}{3}$ j $\frac{2}{3}$

You may have wondered in question **C9** how many places of decimals you need to use when writing a percentage.

$\frac{1}{3}$ as a decimal fraction is 0.333 …
which is 0.33 (correct to 2 decimal places)
and so $\frac{1}{3}$ is 33% (correct to the nearest 1 per cent.)

In the same way if you had to convert 0.336 to a percentage you would get 34% to the nearest 1 per cent.

C10 Express the following decimal fractions as percentages to the nearest 1 per cent:

a   0.462   b   0.589   c   0.666   d   0.209   e   1.389

f   0.8209   g   2.324   h   1.085

C11 Change these to percentages to the nearest 1 per cent:

a $\frac{7}{8}$ b $\frac{5}{6}$ c $1\frac{1}{3}$ d $\frac{4}{15}$ e $\frac{7}{9}$

f $\frac{9}{11}$ g $\frac{20}{22}$ h $3\frac{1}{12}$ i   40   j $\frac{3}{10\,000}$

D   Percentages at work

D1

Jessie has £42.

a   Can she afford to buy the suit?

b   Work out exactly how much she must pay.

c   What change would she get?

You could work out the problem like this:

$$1\% \text{ of } \pounds 56 \quad = \tfrac{1}{100} \times \pounds 56 = \quad 56\text{p}$$

So: $40\% \text{ of } \pounds 56 = 40 \times 56\text{p} = 2\,240\text{p} = \pounds 22.40$

d Jessie decided to offer the shop assistant £22.40. Was she correct? Explain your answer.

D2 Investigate the % key on your calculator.

Try the sequence 5 6 × 4 0 %

Would this help you to solve the last question?

D3 What percentage of £56 should Jessie have calculated to obtain the price she needed to pay? Check using your calculator.

D4 Calculate the following:

a 30% of £90   **b** 10% of £45   **c** 15% of £60

d 5% of £80   **e** 12.5% of £16   **f** $33\tfrac{1}{3}\%$ of £21

D5 Denzil wants to know how far a piece of elastic will stretch beyond its original length. Clare says the increase would be 50%.

a If the elastic was 44 cm long before stretching and 70 cm long when stretched, was Clare correct? Explain your answer.

b Work out the size of Clare's error, if any.

D6 Gareth received £80 for his birthday. He invested it in the Post Office at 5% per annum.

a What does '5% per annum' mean?

b How much interest would Gareth have earned by his next birthday?

UNIT 8 *Algebraic notation and formulae*

The word **ALGEBRA** comes from the title of an Arabic book **AL-JABR WA-AL-MUQABALA** which was written in 820 AD. The title means *the science of cancellation and reduction.*

A Index notation

In arithmetic:
$$2 \times 2 = 2^2$$
$$3 \times 3 = 3^2$$
$$4 \times 4 \times 4 = 4^3 \quad \text{and so on.}$$

Similarly in algebra
$$a \times a = a^2$$
$$a \times a \times a = a^3 \quad \text{and so on.}$$

A1 Simplify these:

a $a \times a$ b $b \times b$ c $a \times a \times a \times a$ d $b \times b \times b$

e $a \times a \times b \times b$ f $g \times h \times g$ g $m^2 \times m^3$ h $a^2 \times a$

i $a \times a \times b$ j $d \times d \times b \times b \times b$

A2 Simplify these:

a $4a \times 2$ b $3x \times x$ c $5a \times a$ d $5a^2 \times a^2$

e $2b \times 2b^2$ f $4x \times 2x$ g $a \div a$

A3 Make a set of cards as shown on the next page. Sort the cards into groups so that, in each group, every card has the same answer. Copy the sets into your book.

A4 With your set of cards, play snap with a friend (you do not need identical cards for saying 'snap' but cards with the same meaning).

Who is right?

A5 Make up a new set of cards and get your friend to sort them into groups of cards having the same answer.

The cards

$s - s$	$2s^2$	one	zero $\times s$
$s \div s$	s	$2 \times s$	$s + s + s$
$2s$	$s \times 0$	$4s$	$s \times s$
$s \times 4$	s^2	$3s$	2
$s \times 2$	$1s$	$\dfrac{s}{s}$	$\dfrac{s}{s} + \dfrac{s}{s}$
$4s^2$	$3 \times s$	zero	$2s - s$
$2s + 2s$	$2s \times 2s$	$2s + s$	$6s - 2s$
s divided by s	half of $2s$	$2ss$	$s + s$

A6 Invent a new game using the set of 32 cards.

B Formulae and substitution

The area of a rectangle is found by multiplying its length by its breadth.
This can be written as:

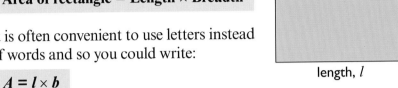

Area of rectangle = Length × Breadth

breadth, *b*

It is often convenient to use letters instead
of words and so you could write:

$$A = l \times b$$

length, *l*

where *A*, *l* and *b* represent the area, length and breadth in appropriate units.

B1   In the formula, find *A* if:

    a $l = 12, b = 5$ **b** $l = 13, b = 7$ **c** $l = 1.5, b = 0.4$

B2   In question **B1**, if *l* and *b* are measured in metres, what will the unit be for *A*?

B3   If $a = 2, b = 3, c = 4, d = 0$, find the values of:

    a $a + b$ **b** $a + b + c$ **c** ab **d** cd

    e $a(b + c)$ **f** $c + ab$ **g** $d(a + b + c)$ **h** $ad + cd$

    i $ab + bc$ **j** $\dfrac{bc}{a}$ **k** $\dfrac{c^2}{a}$ **l** $b^2 - a^2$

B4   If $x = 7, y = 9, z = 13$, find the values of:

    a $3(x + y + z)$ **b** $xy - z$ **c** $z(y - x)$ **d** xyz

    e $3x + 4(z - y)$ **f** $7xz - 9y$ **g** $x^2 + y^2 + z^2$

C Symbols and equations

$$y = \sqrt{7zx}$$

$$e = mc^2$$

$$\frac{4xy}{ab} = z^2$$

$$A = \pi r^2$$

$$T = 2\pi\sqrt{\frac{l}{g}}$$

$$x + 3y = 7$$

$$x^2 + 3y^3 = z^2$$

If you think of a number, add 3 and the answer you get is 11, what was the number you first thought of?

You can write this problem more simply as: $\square + 3 = 11$.

The box takes the place of the number you thought of.

C1 I think of a number, multiply it by 4 and the answer is 12.
Write this problem as above, using a box, then find the number.

C2 In the following, $\square$ stands for a number each time. Find the number:

a $8 + \square = 13$
b $9 + \square = 17$
c $\square + 11 = 20$

d $\square + 12 = 12$
e $14 = \square - 27$
f $20 - \square = 11$

g $\square - 11 = 13$
h $19 - \square = 19$
i $\square - 11 = 0$

j $48 = \square - 2$
k $\frac{10}{\square} = 2$
l $\frac{\square}{7} = 3$

m $3 \times \square = 12$
n $\square \times 9 = 36$
o $\frac{49}{\square} = 7$

C3 Find the values of the symbols in each of these. (Note that if the same symbol is used twice in the same statement it stands for the same number, for example, if $\ast \times \ast = 25$, then $\ast = 5$. The same symbol may, however, have different values in different parts of the question.)

a $\ast + \ast = 36$
b $12 - \# = \#$
c $\bullet + \bullet + \bullet = 24$

d $\blacksquare \times \blacksquare \times \blacksquare = 8$
e $\ast \times \ast = 12 - \ast$
f $\# + \# + \# = 20 + \#$

g $\bullet \times \bullet = \frac{27}{\bullet}$
h $\frac{36}{\blacksquare} = \blacksquare$

C4 If ✶ + # = 17 there are different pairs of values for ✶ and #. For example, ✶ could be 5 and # would then be 12 or ✶ = 2, # = 15 or ✶ = 1, # = 16. Find three pairs of values for the symbols in each of the following:

   a ✶ + # = 12   **b** ■ − 7 = #   **c** $\frac{✶}{●}$ = 20   **d** ■ + ● = 21

   e ✶ − # = 12   **f** $\frac{12}{●}$ = #   **g** ✶ + # = 16   **h** ■ × ● = 16

Here are two computer programs:

Program 1: 10 INPUT L   Program 2: 10 FOR A = 1 to 5

            20 LET M = L + 3   20 B = A * 2

            30 PRINT M   30 PRINT A, B

                                      40 NEXT A

In these programs L, M, A and B stand for numbers in just the same way as the symbols in the last questions. L and A stand for any one of several numbers, M and B stand for just one number at a time depending on the values given to L and A. In the same way we can use letters instead of symbols so that:

$$8 + ✶ = 3$$
Might become $8 + a = 3$

A statement like $8 + a = 3$ is called an **equation**.

C5 Find the values of the letters in the following equations:

   a $5 + a = 19$ **b** $b + 7 = 12$ **c** $17 = a − 9$ **d** $12 − b = 4$

   e $\frac{15}{b} = 3$ **f** $5 × x = 15$ **g** $y − 4 = 8$ **h** $c × c = 9$

In equations like these in parts **f** and **h** above, the multiplication sign × is usually left out. For example:

$5 × x$ is written as $5x$
$c × c$ is written as c^2.

C6 Write the following without the multiplication sign:

   a $7 × x$ **b** $6 × a^2$ **c** $4 × p$ **d** $13 × s$ **e** $11 × a × b$

C7 Find numbers to replace the letters to make these equations true:

   a $5a + 7 = 17$ **b** $2x + 8 = 30$ **c** $6 + 3b = 42$ **d** $19 = 6p + 1$

   e $45 = 5p + 5$ **f** $7a − 6 = 71$ **g** $10p − 5 = 35$ **h** $60 = 5g − 5$

   i $37 = 2q − 3$ **j** $19 − 2p = 3$ **k** $\frac{p}{2} + 6 = 11$ **l** $\frac{t}{3} − 2 = 4$

C8   Look at this program:

```
10 FOR N = 1 TO 5
20 LET T = N + 6
30 PRINT T
40 NEXT N
50 END
```

What does the program do?
What do you expect to be printed out?
Look at line 20: LET T = N + 6

This tells you that T is a number which depends on the value of N.
We call something like T = N + 6 a **formula**.

C9   **Investigation**

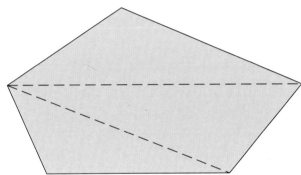

a   Draw a shape like the one above. (It has 5 sides; what is it called?)
Join one corner to all the other corners. There are two lines that are
not sides of the shape and three triangles are formed.

b   Now draw shapes with different numbers of sides and complete the table:

Number of sides	Number of triangles
3	1
4	☐
5	3
6	☐
7	☐
8	☐

c   What is the connection between the number of sides and the number
of triangles formed?
Use S to stand for the number of sides of the shape and T for the
number of triangles formed. Show how the T number is calculated
from the S number.

C10 At a jumble sale a stall is selling magazines at a cost of 8p each. If C is the cost of all the magazines together and n is the number for sale, write a formula for the total cost of all the magazines.

What would the cost be if there were **a** 20 and **b** 12 magazines altogether on the stall?

C11 A child receives 60p pocket money each week and 20p extra for each job done around the house. If T is the total money received and n is the number of jobs done, write a formula to calculate the pocket money.

How much is earned if seven jobs are done?

C12 Pencils cost 13p and pens 19p each. Copy and complete this formula where C = total cost, x = number of pencils and y = number of pens:

$$C = \square\,x + 19\,\square \text{ pence}$$

Use the formula to calculate the cost of six pencils and five pens.

C13

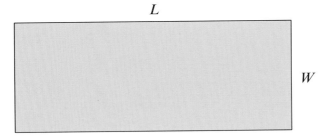

The perimeter of a rectangle is given by the formula:

$$P = 2L + 2W$$

What do the letters P, L and W stand for? Use the formula to find the perimeter of the rectangles below.

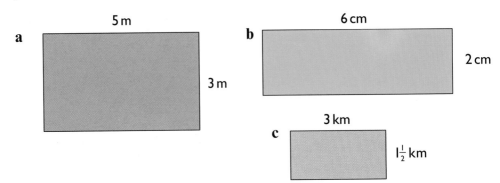

C14 A cookery book gives the time required to cook a joint of meat as:

$T = 20n + 20$

where T is the time in minutes and n is the weight in pounds.

Find the number of minutes needed to cook joints weighing:

a 5 lb   **b** 3 lb   **c** 3.5 lb   **d** 6 lb

If a joint needed exactly an hour to cook, what would be its weight?

C15 The area of a triangle is given by the formula: $A = \frac{1}{2}bh$.

What do the letters A, b and h stand for?

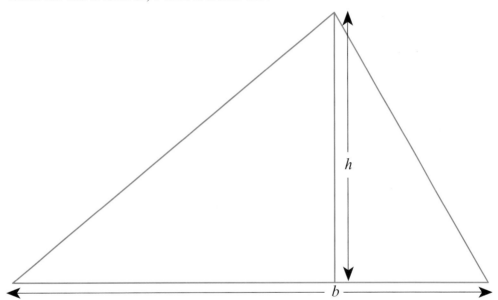

Find the areas of the following triangles:

a $b = 10\,\text{cm}$, $h = 6\,\text{cm}$ **b** $b = 8\,\text{cm}$, $h = 4\,\text{cm}$

c $b = 20\,\text{mm}$, $h = 10\,\text{mm}$ **d** $b = 6\,\text{m}$, $h = 12\,\text{m}$

C16 The cost of hiring a motor bike is £6 per day plus £2 per mile. Which of the following formulae gives the cost and what do the letters represent?

a $C = 6d + 2m$ **b** $C = 2(3d + m)$

c $C = 6d + \frac{m}{2}$ **d** $C = 6d + \frac{2}{m}$

C17 I think of a number, call it n, double it and add 5. The result is P. Which formula gives the relationship between P and n?

a $2n + 5 = P$ **b** $n = 2P - 5$

c $P = 2(n + 2\frac{1}{2})$ **d** $2n - 5 = P$

C18   The connection between degrees Fahrenheit and degrees Celsius is given by:

$F = \frac{9}{5}C + 32$

   a   What is the temperature in degrees Fahrenheit when the Celsius reading is 15°?

   b   What is the temperature in degrees Celsius when the Fahrenheit reading is 104°?

C19   **a** $y = 4x + 7$ find y when $x = 5$

      b $r = 10 + 2b$ find r when $b = 8$

      c $p = 9 - 2s$ find p when $s = 3$

      d $t = 3p + n$ find t when $p = 4$ and $n = 10$

      e $c = \frac{v}{4} + 3$ find c when $v = 12$

      f $a = \frac{b}{c} + d$ find a when $b = 9$, $c = 3$ and $d = 8$

C20   Complete these:

      a $2t + 4t - 3t = \square$ **b** $10a + 5a - 11a = \square$

      c $2p - p - p = \square$ **d** $3b + 2b + 9 = \square$

C21   Copy these and fill in the missing numbers and letters:

      a $2t - 4t + 3t = \square$ **b** $6b - 4b = \square$

      c $9x + \square - 5x = 7x$ **d** $\square + 3t = 9t$

      e $4y - \square + 6y = 8y$ **f** $4d - 4d = \square$

      g $8x + \square = 17x$ **h** $13p - \square = 0$

C22 In each of the following equations, let $x = 2$ and $y = 5$ and work out which are true and which are false:

a $xy = yx$

b $2xy = 2yx$

c $\frac{x}{2} = 1$

d $\frac{xy}{x} = 5$

e $\frac{4y}{x} = 5$

f $\frac{4y}{2x} = 5$

g $\frac{4y}{2} = y$

h $\frac{4y}{4x} = 0$

i $\frac{5}{y} = x - 1$

j $2y = 5x$

C23 Look at this formula: $v = 5s + 7$

Follow these instructions to find v when $s = 2$:

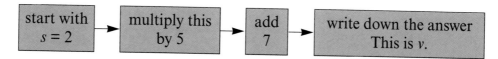

start with $s = 2$ → multiply this by 5 → add 7 → write down the answer This is v.

Now write down similar diagrams for these, giving the answer each time:

a $p = 4t - 3$ and $t = 5$

b $z = x^2 + x + 3$ and $x = 4$

c $y = 3(x + 4)$ and $x = 6$

d $s = 4b + 7$ and $b = 6$

e $b = 10a - 4$ and $a = 3$

f $t = p^2 + 3$ and $p = 4$

g $d = \frac{a}{2} - 6$ and $a = 12$

C24 For each of the tables below, find a rule connecting the two rows and write it in algebraic form.

Petrol used and distance travelled

a
Litres of petrol used, ℓ	0	1	2	3	4	5	6	7	8
Distance travelled, d in miles	0	16	32	48	64				

b
Gallons of petrol used, g	0	1	2	3	4	5	6	7	8
Distance travelled, d in miles	0	47	94	141	188				

Items purchased and cost

c
Number of sweets, s	0	1	2	3	4	5	6	7	8
Cost, c in pence	0	3	6	9	12				

d
Rolls of wallpaper, w	0	1	2	3	4	5	6	7	8
Cost, c in £	0	4	8	12	16				

UNIT 9 *Function machines*

I put x into the machine but didn't get an output.

A Inputs and outputs

Another way of looking at what happens to numbers when they are put into a formula is to use a **function machine**.

A function machine carries out operations, such as multiplication or addition, on numbers. The numbers that are to be operated on form the **input** and the results of the operation give the **output**.

This function machine adds five to the input:

input	function machine	output
x		$x + 5$
7	add 5	12
8		13

and this one divides by 3:

input	function machine	output
x		$\frac{x}{3}$
6	divide by 3	2
9		3

A1   Copy and complete the following:

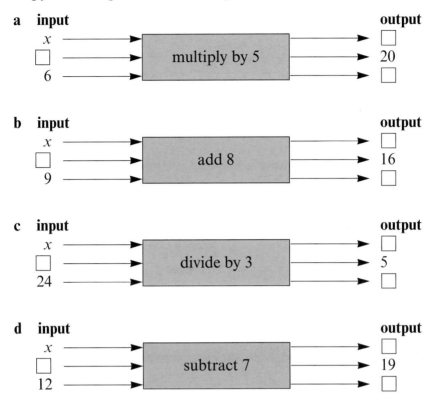

a   input

x →
□ →   multiply by 5   → 20
6 →

output
□
20
□

b   input

x →
□ →   add 8   → 16
9 →

output
□
16
□

c   input

x →
□ →   divide by 3   → 5
24 →

output
□
5
□

d   input

x →
□ →   subtract 7   → 19
12 →

output
□
19
□

A2   Draw some function machines of your own. Write down some inputs and get a friend to work out the outputs.

A3   Suggest what goes in the box in these function machines:

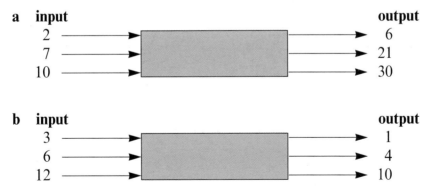

a   input   output
2 →   → 6
7 →   → 21
10 →   → 30

b   input   output
3 →   → 1
6 →   → 4
12 →   → 10

A4   Find **three** different operations which could go into the box in this function machine:

input   output
5 →   → 10

The following function machine performs *two* operations on the input:

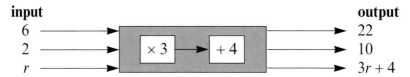

A5   Copy and fill in the gaps for the following function machine:

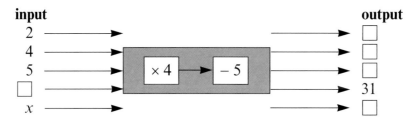

A6   Find the missing operation in each of these function machines:

a

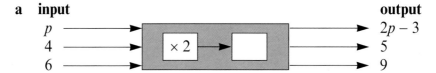

b

A7   Draw some function machines of your own. Put in some inputs and outputs and one of the operations and get a friend to find the missing operation.

A8

Work out the function machine the boys are discussing.

B Function machines in action

Look at this function machine for finding the perimeter of a square:

length of side, l ⟶ $\boxed{\times 4}$ ⟶ perimeter, p

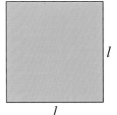

So to find the perimeter of a square when $l = 5$ cm:

Start with 5 ⟶ $\boxed{\times 4}$ ⟶ 20.

Perimeter is 20 cm.

B1 Use the '$\times 4$' function machine to find p when l is:

    a 4 cm   **b** $3\frac{1}{2}$ cm   **c** 5.5 cm   **d** 10 m   **e** 6 mm

You can reverse the function machine to find the length of the side of the square if you know the perimeter. For example, perimeter is 20 cm:

length 5 cm ⟵ $\boxed{\div 4}$ ⟵ start with 20

Notice what happens to '$\times 4$' when you reverse the function machine.

B2

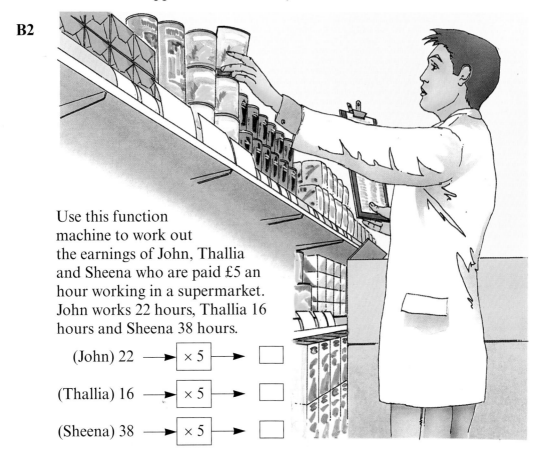

Use this function machine to work out the earnings of John, Thallia and Sheena who are paid £5 an hour working in a supermarket. John works 22 hours, Thallia 16 hours and Sheena 38 hours.

(John) 22 ⟶ $\boxed{\times 5}$ ⟶ $\square$

(Thallia) 16 ⟶ $\boxed{\times 5}$ ⟶ $\square$

(Sheena) 38 ⟶ $\boxed{\times 5}$ ⟶ $\square$

B3   One week each of the employees in question **B2** received their pay packets without the number of hours worked recorded on them. Reverse the function machine to find how many hours were worked by each employee.

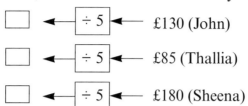

□ ◄— ÷ 5 ◄— £130 (John)

□ ◄— ÷ 5 ◄— £85 (Thallia)

□ ◄— ÷ 5 ◄— £180 (Sheena)

B4   During the sales, a clothes shop cuts the prices of goods to one third of the original price. Find the sales cost of the following:

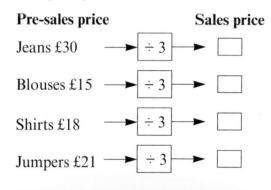

Pre-sales price   **Sales price**

Jeans £30 ——► ÷ 3 ——► □

Blouses £15 ——► ÷ 3 ——► □

Shirts £18 ——► ÷ 3 ——► □

Jumpers £21 ——► ÷ 3 ——► □

B5   Mary wanted some clothes from the sale in question **B4**. Reverse your function machine to find the original price of the clothes that Mary wanted:

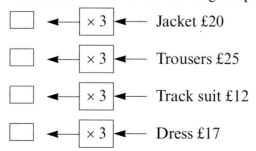

□ ◄— × 3 ◄— Jacket £20

□ ◄— × 3 ◄— Trousers £25

□ ◄— × 3 ◄— Track suit £12

□ ◄— × 3 ◄— Dress £17

B6 Which operation reverses the effect of:

a ×   **b** ÷   **c** +   **d** −

We call these reverse operations **inverses**.

B7 John is 5 years older than his sister Annette. Use a function machine to find John's age when Annette is 13.

(Annette) 13 ⟶ | + 5 | ⟶ ☐ (John)

Reverse the function machine to find Annette's age when John is 24.

(Annette) ☐ ⟵ | − 5 | ⟵ 24 (John)

B8

What are the ages of these two people?

B9 Peter is 7 years younger than Hassan. Use function machines to find Peter's age when Hassan is 26 and Hassan's age when Peter is 22.

B10 Copy and complete the following and draw the inverse operations.

12 ⟶ | − 5 | ⟶ ☐

☐ ⟶ | × 3 | ⟶ 12

7 ⟶ | + ☐ | ⟶ 15

24 ⟶ | ÷ 4 | ⟶ ☐

☐ ⟶ | × 2 | ⟶ 14

B11 Copy and complete the inverse operations on these function machines. The first is done for you:

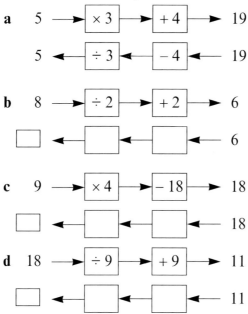

a   5 → × 3 → + 4 → 19

 5 ← ÷ 3 ← − 4 ← 19

b   8 → ÷ 2 → + 2 → 6

 ☐ ← ☐ ← ☐ ← 6

c   9 → × 4 → − 18 → 18

 ☐ ← ☐ ← ☐ ← 18

d 18 → ÷ 9 → + 9 → 11

 ☐ ← ☐ ← ☐ ← 11

B12 Start with a number, call it *n*. Multiply it by 2 and add 7. The answer is 25. What was the number?
Draw a function machine to multiply by 2 and add 7. Reverse the machine and find your mystery number.

B13 Repeat question **B12** with the following numbers and operations:

a start with *n*, multiply by 5, add 6 answer 81

b start with *n*, subtract 3, multiply by 2 answer 8.

B14 If I take my age, multiply it by 3 and subtract 7, I get the answer 164. How old am I?

B15 Make up three function machine of your own (like the ones in question **B11**). Give them to a friend and see if they can produce correct function machines to work backwards.

C Graphs of inputs and outputs

You can draw a *graph* of the input and output from a function machine and then use the graph to find the output of any input you wish.

For example, a $\boxed{\times 4}$ machine:

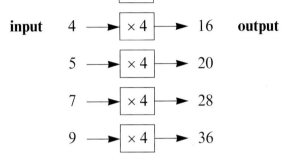

C1

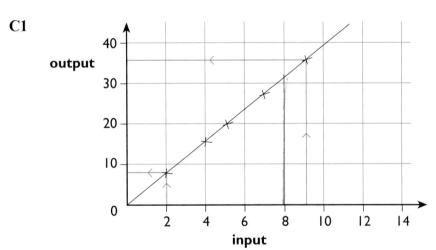

Use centimetre squared paper. Draw horizontal and vertical axes, using a scale of 1 cm to 2 units on the horizontal axis and 1 cm to 10 units on the vertical axis. Plot the input and output as pairs of coordinates on your graph:

(4,16) (5,20) (7,28) (9,36)

To find the output when the input is 2, draw a line from 2 on the input axis to the graph line, then across to the output axis. You should find an input of 2 gives an output of 8. Similarly check that an input of 10 gives an output of 40.

C2   From your graph, find outputs for inputs of:

a 0   **b** 5   **c** 8

C3 **a** Copy and complete these machines:

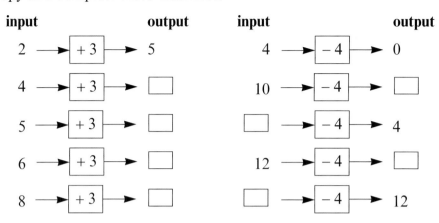

b Write down the input and output as ordered pairs in each case in part **a**. For example:

+3 machine: (2,5) (4,☐) and so on.

−4 machine: (4,0) and so on.

c Now plot a graph for each machine in part **a**.

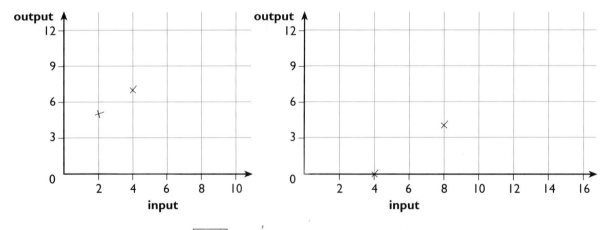

d From the +3 machine graph, find the output for inputs of:

i 3   **ii** 5   **iii** 9   **iv** 6.5   **v** 3.5

e From the −4 machine graph, find the output for inputs of:

i 6   **ii** 9   **iii** 14   **iv** 12.5   **v** 4.5

C4 See if you can use your graphs in question **C3** 'backwards' to find inputs if you know outputs. What would be the inputs for each of the machines if the outputs are:

a 6   **b** 3   **c** 9   **d** 0   **e** 8   **f** 5.5   **g** 10

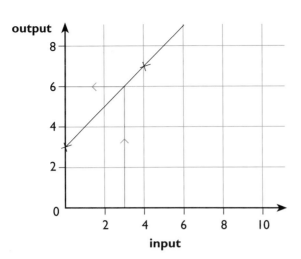

Graph for ⊞ + 3 ⊞ machine showing output of 6 coming from input of 3.

C5 Using inputs of 0, 2, 3, 5, 6 for a ⊞ + 5 ⊞ machine, write down five ordered pairs and plot them on a graph. Use your graph to find:

a the outputs for inputs of: 4   8   7.

b the inputs for outputs of: 12   9   6.

C6 Choosing your own inputs (don't make the numbers too large!) write down five ordered pairs for the machines:

a ⊞ − 3 ⊞   **b** ⊞ × 2 ⊞   **c** ⊞ + 7 ⊞

and draw the graph in each case.

C7 Copy and complete:

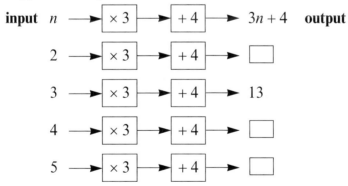

List the inputs and outputs above as ordered pairs and then plot them on a graph using 1 cm for each unit on the horizontal axis and 1 cm for 5 units on the vertical scale.
Use your graph to find the output when the input is:

a 1   **b** 6   **c** 2.5   **d** 0

What is the input if the output is:

a 25   **b** 22   **c** 4?

UNIT 10 *Equations*

A Using flowcharts

In Unit 8 you looked at problems like these:

Three more than a number is 15, find the number.

Four times a number minus 11 is 43, find the number.

If you call the unknown numbers a and b you get:

$a + 3 = 15$ and $4b - 11 = 43$

When you find the answers for a and b you have *solved* the equations.

A1 Using trial and error, solve these equations:

    a $2a + 4 = 22$ **b** $5p - 7 = 53$ **c** $4t + 10 = 46$ **d** $5x + 2 = 57$

A more systematic way to solve equations is to use **flowcharts**.
For example, to solve:

$3n - 11 = 25$

| start with n | → | multiply by 3 | → | subtract 11 | → | answer is 25 |

Now reverse:

| answer is $n = 12$ | ← | divide by 3 | ← | add 11 | ← | start with 25 |

A2 Use flowcharts to solve these equations:

    a $2b + 7 = 31$ **b** $5d - 9 = 41$ **c** $13 + 6a = 25$ **d** $2t - 8 = 67$

A3 Here is a problem: 'In a box of chocolates, the number of chocolates with hard centres is h and the number with soft centres is 9. How many chocolates will have hard centres in three boxes containing a total of 60 chocolates?'

The total number of chocolates can be written as an equation, as follows:

$3(h + 9) = 60$

To solve this equation it is necessary to get rid of the brackets first, to give:

$3h + 27 = 60$

Solve the equation above using a flowchart.

A4 Solve these equations using flowcharts:

   a $2(p + 4) = 18$ **b** $7(4 + t) = 49$ **c** $5(b - 2) = 30$

   d $4(9 - g) = 28$ **e** $3(8 + r) = 39$ **f** $9(12 - m) = 63$

B Using letters

Another way of solving equations is to think of a balanced weighing scale. Look at this picture.

The scales balance so the pot weighs 40 g.

B1   **a**   What does this pot weigh?

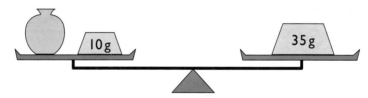

   b   If you take the 10 g weight from the left pan, what must be taken from the right pan to make the scales balance?

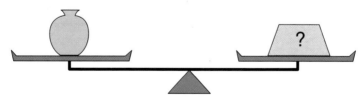

B2   What must be put in the right pan to keep things balanced?

B3

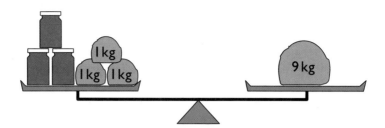

Remove 3 kg from each pan.
How much does each jar weigh if the jars all have the same weight?

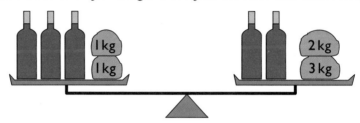

If the bottles in the picture above each weigh p kg
and the scales balance, then: $3p + 2 = 2p + 5$

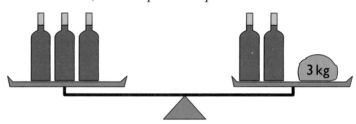

So, taking 2 kg from each side: $3p = 2p + 3$

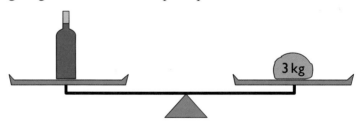

and, taking two bottles from each side: $p = 3$
So each bottle weighs 3 kg.

B4   If 4 bottles and three 2 kg weights balance exactly with 2 bottles and two
4 kg weights, what does each bottle weigh?

B5   If 5 jars and six 3 kg weights balance exactly with 7 jars, five 3 kg weights
and one 2 kg weight, what does each jar weigh?

B6   A set of identical triplets all have exactly the same weight. They stand on
a see-saw together and are balanced by their father who weighs 78 kg.
How much does each triplet weigh?

The picture above illustrates the equation: $b + 3 = 15$
To solve the equation and keep the scales balanced,
you **take away** 3 from each side.
So $b = 12$.

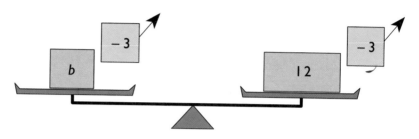

To solve an equation of this type: $c - 5 = 16$
you need to **add** 5 to each side.

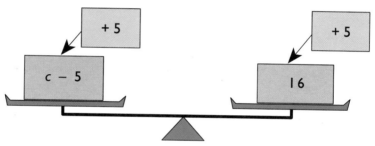

So $c = 21$.

B7 Use the balance method above to solve these equations:

a $4a + 3 = 51$ b $b + 7 = 15$ c $2a + 3 = 15$

d $3a + 2 = 8 + a$ e $c - 7 = 12$ f $d - 5 = 23$

B8 Solve these equations:

a $p - 2 = 71$ b $q + 3 = 43$ c $2r - 7 = 15$

d $s + 7 = 2s + 3$ e $t - 11 = 94$ f $3t = 51$

When solving equations, you do not need to *draw* a balance every time.

What is important is that you keep the equation **balanced**.

To do this you must always **do the same operation to *both sides* of the equation**.

Here are some examples:

To solve $b + 7 = 15$

Subtract 7 from each side: $b + 7 - 7 = 15 - 7$

To give $b = 8$

To solve $2a + 3 = 17$

Subtract 3 from each side: $2a + 3 - 3 = 17 - 3$

To give: $2a = 14$

Divide both sides by 2: $a = 7$

To solve $3a + 2 = 8 + a$

Subtract 2 from each side: $3a + 2 - 2 = 8 + a - 2$

To give: $3a = 6 + a$

Subtract a from both sides: $2a = 6$

Divide both sides by 2: $a = 3$

B9   Solve these equations:

a $2x + 3 = 18$ **b** $3y - 4 = 14$ **c** $2(a + 5) = 18$

d $27 = 3p$ **e** $25 = 3c + 4$ **f** $24 + a = 5a + 8$

g $3z + 7 = 46$ **h** $9p - 16 = 29$ **i** $17 + t = 2t + 2$

In each case check your answer by putting the value you find back in the equation and making sure it balances.

B10

When Gail divided her 23 sweets among her four friends there were three sweets left for her. Let *s* be the number of sweets each friend received. Write down an equation involving *s* and then solve it. How many sweets did each friend receive?

B11 I divide a number by 6 and add 3. The answer is 8. What is the number? (Call the number '*x*', write down an equation and solve it.)

B12 Three more than twice a number is 21. What is the number? Answer this question using equations.

B13 Solve these equations:

a $4n + 5 = 9$ b $3n = 12 - n$ c $16 = 2a - 4$

d $\frac{2n}{3} = 4$ e $\frac{4a}{2} - 6 = 18$ f $3n + 6 = 26 - n$

g $7k - 32 = 66$ h $\frac{5s}{12} = 10$ i $m - 0.5 = 2m + 1.5$

B14 If Tom multiplies his house number by 3 and then adds 9, he gets exactly ten times his sister's age. His sister's age is the answer to the equation:

$7s - 12 = 30$

What is Tom's house number?

B15 On Monday I bought 3 cups of coffee and received £2.90 change from £5. What does a cup of coffee cost? Solve this:

a   using an equation   b   without using algebra.

B16 Make up some equations of your own and solve them.

Also swap your equations with a friend and solve each other's equations. Check that you get the same answers

B17   Amina has three packets of biscuits and two extra biscuits. John has two packets of the same biscuits and 18 extra ones. If they both have the same number of biscuits write down an equation and use it to find:

    a   how many biscuits there are in a packet

    b   how many biscuits Amina and John have each?

B18   Steven took out some pencils from his desk. Three pencils remained in the desk. Altogether there were 14 pencils. Write down an equation and solve it to find how many he took out.

B19   I think of a number, add 3, multiply by 12 and the answer is 240. Write down an equation and find the number.

B20   I buy some light bulbs. If I had bought three more, then twice the total bought would have been three times the number actually bought plus 1.

Write down an equation and use it to find how many light bulbs I bought.

C Equations everywhere

C1 Solve these equations and complete the number 'crossword' below:

Clues across

1 $5n = 200$
2 $3x + 1 = 4$
3 $2n - 3 = 19$
5 $a + 7 = 29$
6 $2 + a = 29$
7 $2n - 1 = 19$
8 $2a + 3 = \boxed{}$ when $a = 3$
9 $n - 5 = 107$
10 $\frac{n}{2} = 32$
12 $4n = 80$
14 $3t + 7 = 43$
16 $\frac{2n}{5} + 1 = 7$
17 $5x - 9 = 51$
18 $\frac{3n}{4} + 8 = 17$

Clues down

1 $b - 3 = 45$
2 $z - 2 = 10$
3 $2x + 6 = 30$
4 $p + 9 = 26$
5 $4a + 2 = \boxed{}$ when $a = 50$
7 $g + 7 = 18$
11 $5b + 4 = \boxed{}$ when $b = 8$
12 $\frac{n}{2} + 3 = 108$
13 $5x + 3 = 28$
14 $5a + 1 = 56$
15 $6y + 4 = \boxed{}$ when $y = 3$

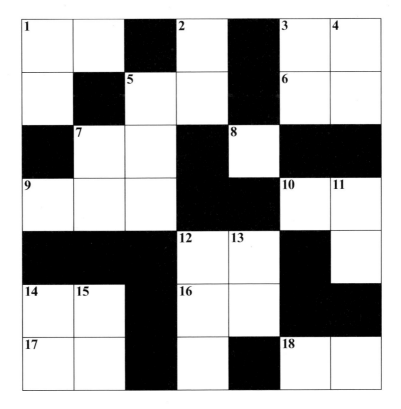

C2   The answers to these equations follow a pattern.

Solve the equations and find the pattern.

   a $6x + 7 = 13$

   b $3y + 9 = 17 + y$

   c $16 - 2z = z - 11$

   d $1.5z - 3 = 21$

   e $z + 0.2z = 30$

   f Make up an equation which gives the next number in the pattern as an answer.

C3   Solve these equations and, as in question **C2**, see if you can spot a pattern.

   a $2z + 11 = 33$

   b $3z + 22 = 55$

   c $4z + 33 = 77$

   d $99 - z = 88$

   e $111 + z = 222$

   f $2222 + z = 3333$

C4

$$2x + 27 = x + 33 + x$$

Ali is having trouble solving this equation – can you see what his problem is?

C5 The solutions to the following problems will spell out a message if you use the code:

$1 = A$ $2 = B$ $3 = C$ $4 = D$ and so on up to $25 = Y$ $26 = Z$

Solve the problems and find the message.

a $3x + 10$ when $x = 5$

b   when multiplied by itself this number gives 225

c $a + b - c$ when $a = 37$, $b = 51$ and $c = 67$

d $x^2 + y^2 - z^2 + 1$ when $x = 4$, $y = 3$, $z = 5$

e $0.5n - 12$ when $n = 60$

f $3p - 7 = p + 3$

g $z^2 - 166$ when $z = 13$

h $\frac{k}{144}$ when $k = 1728$

i $q + 3 = 3q - 7$

j $\frac{h}{k}$ when $h = 444\,444$ and $k = 20\,202$

k $r + 7 = 3r - 3$

l $\frac{(m - 24)}{2}$ when $m = 60$

C6

Make up a problem like this yourself and ask a friend to solve it.

UNIT 11 *Graphs and formulae*

A Making formulae and drawing graphs

In a factory, dolls are assembled from arms, bodies, heads and legs. A skilled worker can assemble 30 dolls in an hour.

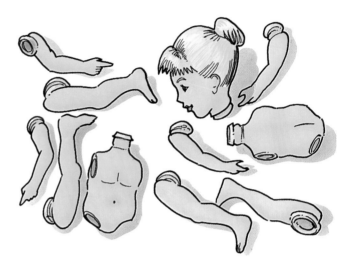

A1 How many could be assembled in

a 2 hours   **b** 3 hours?

Copy and complete this table:

Number of hours worked	1	2	3	4	5	6	7	8
Number of dolls made	30							

You can represent the relationship between these two sets of numbers in several ways:

1 As a set of *ordered pairs*: (1,30) (2,60) (3,90) …

2 Using a *function machine*:

input 1 ————→ ×30 ————→ 30 **output**
         2 ————→   ————→ 60
        etc.   etc.

3 As a *statement*: The number of dolls is 30 times the number of hours.

4 As a *formula*: $d = 30n$
where d = number of dolls and n = number of hours.

A2 **a** Plot the ordered pairs in question **A1** on a graph. Let 2 cm represent 1 hour on the x-axis and $\frac{1}{2}$ cm represent 10 dolls on the y-axis.

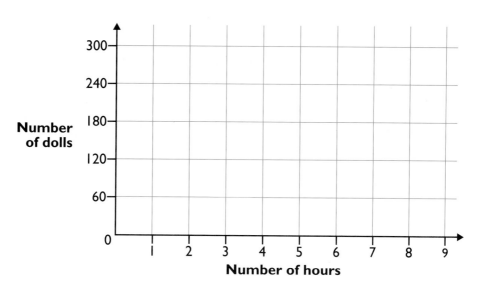

b Copy and complete the following ordered pairs and then plot them on your graph:

$(\frac{1}{2},\square)$ $(1\frac{1}{2},\square)$ $(2\frac{1}{2},\square)$ … up to $(8\frac{1}{2},\square)$

Join up all your plotted points.

Does the point (0,0) belong to the line?

c Is it true that for every point on the line the y-coordinate is always 30 times the x-coordinate?

Can you answer the question?

A company hires out equipment to the public. The cost of hire is given by the formula:

$C = dn + 10$

where:

C = total cost in £
n = number of days of hiring
d = hire rate in £ per day.

So, for example, the cost of hiring a large ladder at £5 per day for 3 days is:

$C = 3 \times 5 + 10 = £25$

A3 Find the cost of hiring a ladder at £5 per day for:

a 6 days   **b** 11 days.

A4 For how many days is the ladder hired (at £5 per day) if the total cost is:

a £35   **b** £55   **c** £50?

Here is part of a
hire charge sheet:

> **The fixed charge on all items is
> £10 + rate below:**
>
> **Carpet cleaner . . . . £4 per day**
> **Electric saw . . . . £4.20 per day**
> **Extending ladder . . . . £9 per day**
> **Paint stripper . . . . £5.50 per day**
> **Sanding machine. . . . . £3 per day**
> **Scaffolding . . . . £20 per day**
> **Sharpening equipment . . £3.10 per day**
> **Straight ladders: large . . . . £5 per day**
> **   small . . . . £3 per day**

A5 Using the formula: $C = dn + 10$
work out the cost of hiring the following equipment:

a paint stripper for 2 days

b extending ladder and an electric saw for 7 days

c small straight ladder and an electric saw for 7 days

d carpet cleaner for 1 day

e scaffolding for 14 days.

A6 Write the hire charge for a carpet cleaner for 1 to 10 days as ordered pairs:

(1,14) (2,18) … up to (10,50)

Now plot these ordered pairs on a graph like the one below. (Use a scale of 1 day = 2 cm and £2 = 1 cm.)

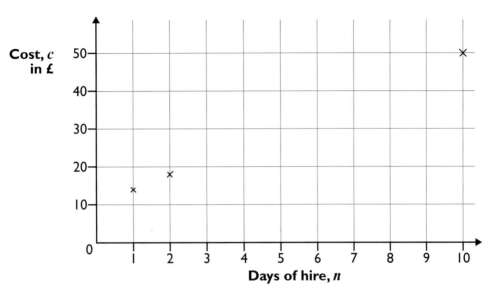

On the same graph, and using different colours, plot the cost of hiring:

a the sanding machine **b** the paint stripper.

A7 A fairground wheel makes 6 turns every minute. Copy and complete this table:

Number of minutes	$\frac{1}{2}$	1	$1\frac{1}{2}$	2	$2\frac{1}{2}$	3	$3\frac{1}{2}$	4	$4\frac{1}{2}$	5	$5\frac{1}{2}$
Number of turns		6	9								

a Plot these ordered pairs on a graph.
Join up the plotted points.
What sort of graph do you get?

b What is the relationship between the x- and y-coordinates?

c What is the formula that connects the time and the number of turns?

B Plotting graphs

B1   Which of these ordered pairs belong to the graph of the formula: $y = 2x + 1$
(0,1) (2,5) (4,9) (5,11) (6,14) (8,19)?

First write down which ordered pairs belong, then draw the graph and plot their positions to check if you were correct.

B2   Which of these ordered pairs belong to the graph of: $y = x - 1$
(1,0) (2,1) (4,3) (5,4) (7,6) (9,8)

First write down which ordered pairs belong, then draw the graph and plot their positions to check if you were correct.

B3   Write down the coordinates of the points
A, B, C, D, E, F, G.
What is the y-coordinate for each point?
We could say that the formula for the line was:
$y = \square$.
Fill in the missing number.

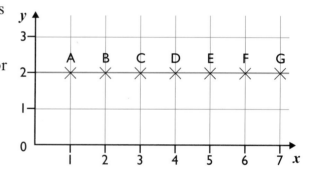

B4   Write down the coordinates of the points P, Q, R, S, T.
What do they have in common?
What do you think is the formula for the line?

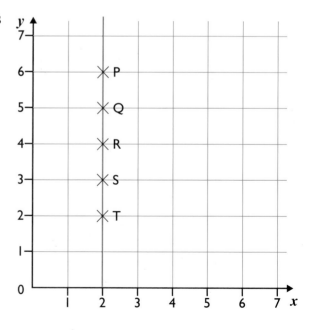

B5   Copy and complete the following:

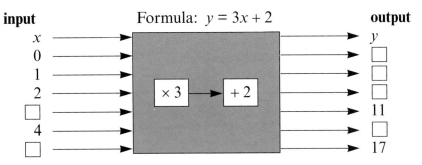

input   Formula: $y = 3x + 2$ **output**

Write each input and output as an ordered pair.
Using centimetre squared paper, draw an x-axis with a scale from 0 to 6
and a y-axis with a scale from 0 to 20.
Plot the ordered pairs and join up the plotted points.

B6   Draw an x-axis and label it from 0 to 6 using a scale of 2 cm for 1 unit
and a y-axis and label it from 0 to 10 using the same scale.

Plot these ordered pairs: (0,0) (1,1) (2,2) (3,3) (4,4) (5,5).
Join them up.
What formula do you think connects x and y?

B7   Repeat question **B6** using the ordered pairs:

(0,0) (1,2) (2,4) (3,6) (4,8).

B8   Draw x- and y-axes with each axis numbered from 0 to 20 using a scale
of 1 cm = 1 unit. On these axes, plot graphs for the following formulae.
First make up a table, then list the ordered pairs and put them on a
graph. Finally join the plotted points and put the name against the
graph. (Use different colours for each one.)

In part **a**, the table and coordinates are done for you. You should do
parts **b** to **e** like this.

a $y = x$

x	0	1	2	3	4	5	6	7	8	9	10
y	0	1	2	3	4	5	6	7	8	9	10

    (0,0) (1,1) (2,2) (3,3) (4,4) (5,5) (6,6) (7,7) (8,8) (9,9) (10,10)

b $y = 2x$ (take x from 0 to 10)   **c** $y = 3x$ (take x from 0 to 5)

d $y = \frac{1}{2}x$ (take x from 0 to 20)   **e** $y = \frac{1}{4}x$ (take x from 0 to 20)

Look carefully at the graphs you have drawn.
Describe anything you notice.

Here are some things you might have noted about your graphs on the last page:

1. Every graph is a straight line (this is called a **linear** graph).
2. Each graph goes through the point (0,0).
3. From left to right each graph goes 'up hill'.
4. The slope of each graph is different.

B9 Write down the names of the graphs in order of steepness:

Steepest: $y = 3x$
$\qquad\qquad y = \ldots\ldots$
$\qquad\qquad y = \ldots\ldots$
$\qquad\qquad y = \ldots\ldots$
Least steep: $y = \ldots\ldots$

If you wanted to draw $y = 2.5x$, between which two lines would it go?

B10 For the following formulae, make up a table, write down coordinates and plot the graphs, in the same way as in question **B8**.

a $y = x + 0$ **b** $y = x + 3$ **c** $y = x + 5$

Plot each graph in a different colour and label carefully.

What is special about the lines you get?
What is the connection between the formula and the point where a line cuts the y-axis?

Suggest where the graph of $y = x + 2$ should be and then draw it to check whether you were correct.

B11   **Extension**
Repeat question **B10** for the following graphs using values of x from 0 to 10:

a $y = x - 2$ **b** $y = x - 4$ **c** $y = x - 1$

What happens to some values of y when you make up a table?

Describe how you can cope with the problem on your axes before you draw the graphs.

C Drawing graphs with a computer

C1   Using **BASIC** on the computer, try this program:

```
10 MODE 1
20 MOVE 0,100
30 FOR X = 40 TO 400 STEP 40
40 LET Y = 2 * X + 100
50 DRAW X,Y
60 NEXT X
70 END
```

Now draw the graph yourself. Make a table:

$y = 2x + 100$

x	0	40	80	120	... up to ...	360	400
y	100	180					900

Then plot points (0,100) (40,180) ... choosing scales as shown on the next page.

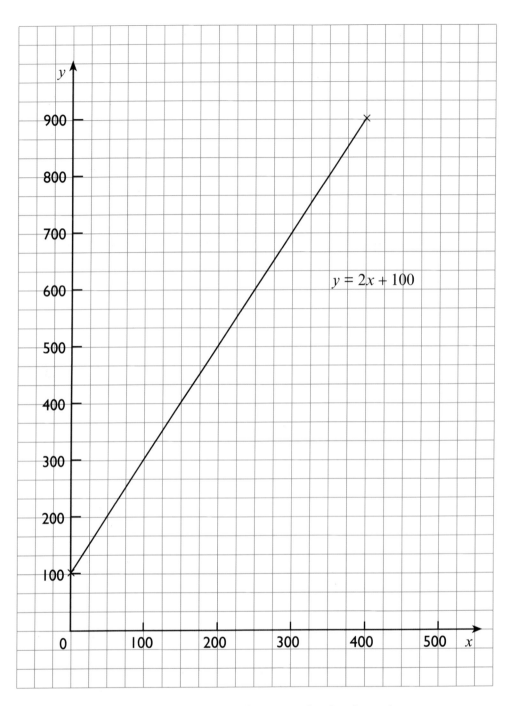

Compare your graph with the one that you obtained on the computer.
For both graphs:

1. The equation is $y = 2x + 100$.
2. The points lie on a straight line.
3. The line cuts the y-axis at (0,100).
4. The slope is the same.

C2 Put this program into the computer:

```
10 MODE 1                              100 DRAW X,Y
20 MOVE 0,100                          110 NEXT X
30 FOR X = 40 TO 400 STEP 40           120 MOVE 0,500
40 Y = 2*X + 100                       130 FOR X = 40 TO 400 STEP 40
50 DRAW X, Y                           140 Y = 2*X + 500
60 NEXT X                              150 DRAW X,Y
70 MOVE 0,300                          160 NEXT X
80 FOR X = 40 TO 400 STEP 40           170 END
90 Y = 2*X + 300
```

Try to answer these questions *before* you run the program:

a How many graphs are plotted?
b What is the formula for each?
c What are the coordinates of the first point plotted by the program on each graph?
d What can you say about the graphs?

Now run the program and notice what you get. Draw the graphs in your book using the same axes as in question **C1**.

C3 Look at this program:

```
10 MODE 1                              100 DRAW X,Y
20 MOVE 0,400                          110 NEXT X
30 FOR X = 40 TO 400 STEP 40           120 MOVE 0,400
40 Y = X + 400                         130 FOR X = 40 TO 400 STEP 40
50 DRAW X, Y                           140 Y = 3*X + 400
60 NEXT X                              150 DRAW X,Y
70 MOVE 0,400                          160 NEXT X
80 FOR X = 40 TO 400 STEP 40           170 END
90 Y = 2*X + 400
```

Before you run the program, try to work out what it does.
a What straight lines does it draw?
b Where do the lines cut the y-axis?
c What do you notice about the slopes of the lines?

Now run the program and make a note of what you get.

C4 Explore these groups of graphs. You will need to write your own programs like the ones in the questions above.

a $y = x + 200$ $y = 2x + 200$ $y = 3x + 200$

b $y = 2x$ $y = 2x - 100$ $y = 2x + 100$

c $y = 3x$ $y = 3x + 400$ $y = 3x - 400$

UNIT 12 *Investigations and formulae*

A Carrying out an investigation

 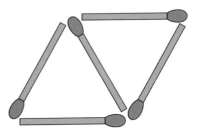

How many matchsticks are used to make these shapes? They are the start of a sequence of shapes based on triangles. You could investigate how many matchsticks are needed to make 1, 2, 3, etc. triangles.

Here is a set of steps to remember when doing an investigation like this one:

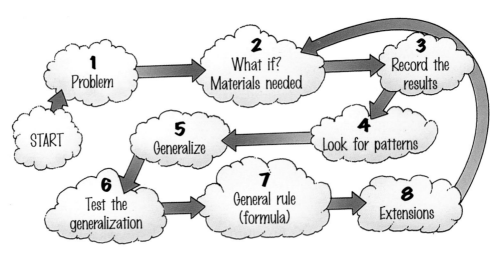

You should go through as many of these steps as possible.

Looking at the steps

1 **The problem**: to find the number of matchsticks needed to make different numbers of triangles.

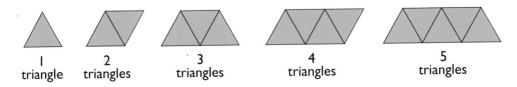

| 1 triangle | 2 triangles | 3 triangles | 4 triangles | 5 triangles |

2   **What if?** What if you started with the simplest triangle?
    Materials needed: matchsticks and paper.

3   **Record the results**: usually by means of a table.

Number of triangles, n	Number of matchsticks, T	Add on
1	3	2
2	5	2
3	7	2
4	9	2
5	11	2
6	13	2

4   **Look for patterns**: from one line to the next you add 2.
    So 7 triangles need 15 matches
        8 triangles need 17 matches and so on ...

5   **Generalize**: what is the connection between the number of triangles
    and the number of matchsticks?
    6 triangles need 13 matches, 7 need 15 and so on.
    The rule might be 'multiply number of triangles by 2 and add 1'.

6   **Test the generalization**.
    Check (say) the case with 20 triangles, you should need
    $40 + 1 = 41$ matches.
    Check that this is correct. Try a few other numbers.

7   **General rule** (formula):
    number of matchsticks = 2 × number of triangles + 1
    So: $T = 2n + 1$.
    Check that this works. For example, if $n = 5$, $T = 11$. Correct!

8   **Extensions**:
    What about different shapes, for example, squares.

A1

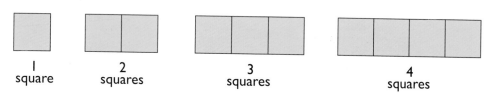

| 1 | 2 | 3 | 4 |
| square | squares | squares | squares |

Work you way through the eight steps, doing the investigation for squares.
Can you find a formula?

Can you suggest any further extensions?

A2   Investigate even and odd numbers. Work you way through the eight steps and keep a note of what you do.

Even numbers

Order		Value
first	1	2
second	2	4
third	3	6
fourth	4	8
hundredth	100	☐
nth	n	☐

Odd numbers

Order	Value
1	1
2	3
3	5
4	7
100	☐
n	☐

Find a formula for:

a   the nth even number

b   the nth odd number.

A3   Investigate this pattern.

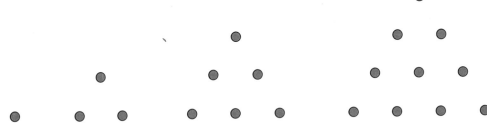

Work through the eight steps and try to find a formula which will give the number of dots in any triangle.

A4

I'm going to investigate the number of ways I can arrange the letters in my name.

Easy, it must be the same as mine, 12.

JANE

BILL

Investigate Bill's claim. Is he correct?

A5   Investigate how many lines are required to join a number of dots together.

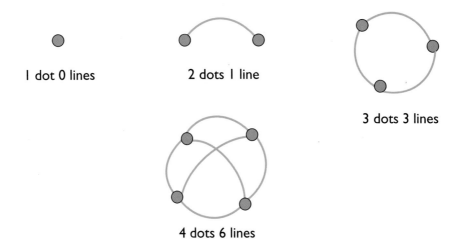

Work through all the eight steps and make a note of what you do at each step.

See if you can find a formula connecting the number of dots and the number of lines.

Suggest any extensions to this investigation.

A6   For this investigation you may find it useful to use dotty paper, squared paper or even cubes.

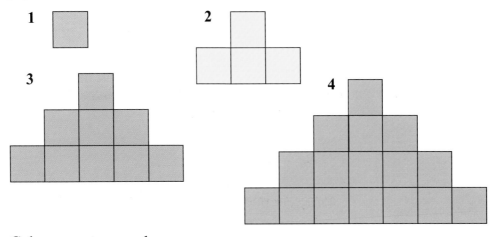

Cubes are set up as shown.
Find the number of cubes in:

a   the 6th shape.

b   the 100th shape.

c   Find a formula for the number of cubes in the *n*th shape.

It may help if you think about how many cubes are in the bottom row each time.

Work through the eight steps and keep a note of what you do.

A7

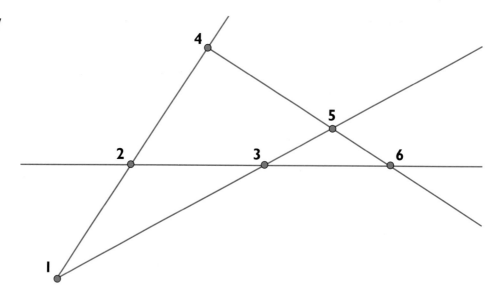

This picture shows 4 lines and there are 6 points of intersection.

Draw any number of lines. Make them all cross each other. Keep a note of:

● the number of lines
● the number of points where they cross.

See if you can find a formula connecting the number of lines and the number of crossings.

Using differences

Sometimes it is difficult to know whether a set of numbers form a sequence with a general rule. Try using the *method of differences* to help you.

For example, for this sequence:

6   7   11   18   28   41   ...

you could work as follows:

1   Write down the sequence.
2   Write down the differences between consecutive numbers.
3   Write out the differences between these new numbers.

And so on ... .

For the sequence above you would get:

	6		7		11		18		28		41	...
differences		1		4		7		10		13		
differences			3		3		3		3			

You can see that there is a pattern and could work backwards to find the next number:

```
6    7    11    18    28    41   (57)
   1    4    7    10    13   (16)
      3    3    3    3    (3)
```

so the next number in the sequence is 57.

To get this you put an extra 3 in the bottom line and work upwards, first adding it to 13 to get 16 and then adding 16 to 41 to get 57.

You could go on getting more numbers in the sequence in the same way.

A8 Use the method of differences to suggest a value for the next number in each of these sequences:

a   1   3   9   27   81

b   3   8   15   24   35   48

c   6   11   18   27   38   51   66

d   2   5   10   17   26   37   50

e   6   10   16   24   34   46   60

f   37   34   31   28   25   22

g   2   9   28   65   126   217

h   1   7   13   19   25   31

A9 Find the output from the following programs and investigate the sequences produced?

a
```
10 FOR NUMBER = 1 TO 10
20 PRINT 4*NUMBER
30 NEXT NUMBER
40 END
```

b
```
10 FOR NUMBER = 1 TO 15
20 PRINT 6*NUMBER
30 NEXT NUMBER
40 END
```

A10 Make up programs to produce the following sequences by making use of the differences:

a   1   4   7   10   13

b   2   7   12   17   22

c   5   8   11   14   17

d   3   7   11   15   19

e   1   5   9   13   17   21

f   4   7   10   13   16   19

The market, madam? Get off at the nth bus stop.

B Problems

B1 Investigate the following problem and try to work out a general formula.

At its first stop a bus picks up one passenger, at its second stop three passengers, at its third stop five passengers and so on.

a How many passengers are picked up at the ninth stop? How many at the nth stop?

b At the first stop there was one passenger already on the bus. How many passengers were on the bus after stop 2, stop 3, etc.?

c How many will there be after the nth stop?

d When do you think the bus will be full? Explain your answer.

B2

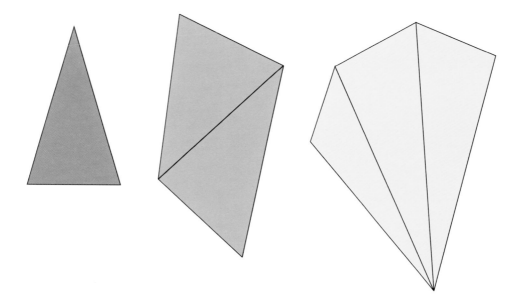

You can divide figures like the ones above into triangles.

Make a table with the following headings:

Number of sides	Number of vertices	Number of triangles

Work through the eight steps of an investigation on page 111 to find formulae for the numbers of vertices and triangles in terms of the number of sides.

B3   Below are the formulae for the *n*th terms of several sequences. In each case find the values of:

  i   1st and 2nd terms
  ii   3rd and 4th terms
  iii 10th term
  iv   100th term

  a $V = n + 4$

  b $V = n^2 + n$

  c $V = n^2 - n$

  d $V = \frac{1}{n}$

  e $V = n^2 + 1$

  f $V = 2n^2$

B4   Match the sequences **a** – **f** below to the correct formula **A** – **F**.
For example, sequence **a** matches formula **c**.

Sequences:

a	1	2	3	4	5	6	...
b	1	3	5	7	9	11	...
c	2	4	6	8	10	12	...
d	2	7	12	17	22	27	...
e	-2	1	6	13	22	33	...
f	2	4	8	16	32	64	...

Formulae:

A $y = 5x - 3$

B $y = 2n$

C $y = n$

D $y = 2^n$

E $y = 2n - 1$

F $y = x - 3$

B5   Work out formulae for the following sequences:

   a   2   3   4   5   6   7   ...

   b   3   5   7   9   11   13   ...

   c   3   4   5   6   7   8   ...

   d   5   7   9   11   13   ...

   e   4   6   8   10   12   ...

   f   8   16   32   64   128   ...

   g   8   10   12   14   16   ...

   h   4   8   16   32   64   ...

B6   The following pictures represent pentagonal numbers. Find the 5th
pentagonal number.

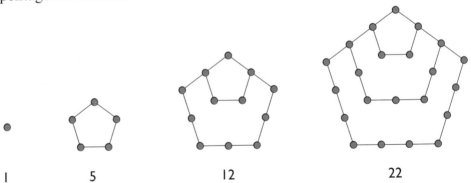

1   5   12   22

Using the eight steps for an investigation, try to discover a pattern for
these numbers.

Try to find a rule and a formula.

B7   Hexagons are joined together along their edges as shown.

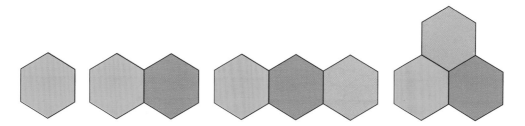

For different numbers of hexagons, find the arrangement which gives the largest perimeter.

Copy and complete this table:

Number of hexagons	1	2	3	4	5	6
Largest possible perimeter			14			

Can you find a formula?

Investigate arrangements giving the smallest possible perimeter.

B8   Draw some shapes on dotty paper using straight lines so that there is always exactly one dot inside the shape.

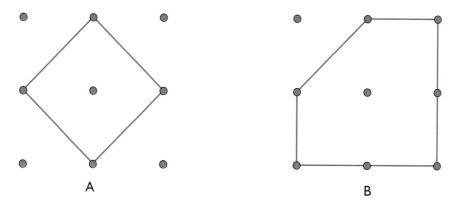

Shape A has 4 dots on the perimeter and area 2 units.
Shape B has 7 dots on the perimeter and area $3\frac{1}{2}$ units.

Investigate the relationship between the number of dots on the perimeter and the area.

Number and algebra 2
National Curriculum
level description coverage

NC level description	Covered in pupil's book unit:
● use the understanding of place value to multiply and divide whole numbers and decimals by 10, 100 and 1000	2, 6, 7
● order, add and subtract negative numbers in context	4, 6
● use all four operations with decimals to two places	7
● calculate fractional or percentage parts of quantities and measurements using a calculator where appropriate	1, 2, 7
● understand and use an appropriate non-calculator method for solving problems that involve multiplying and dividing any three-digit by any two-digit number	3
● check solutions by applying inverse operations or estimating using approximations	6, 7, 9
● construct, express in symbolic form and use simple formulae involving one or two operations	5, 8, 9, 10, 11, 12
● using and applying the above skills	All units